Study Guide

& the
Secret of the
Hidden
Cave

Table of Contents

Getting the Most From This Study Guide

The Jonathan Park Audio Adventures were produced to help children and families have a strong foundation in which to build their faith! Unfortunately many live as if their belief in the Bible is just another brand of religion. However, God has given us a gift that we often take for granted – He has asked us to believe in truth! Sadly, many Christians are intimidated by evolutionary ideas and told that the Word of God has been disproven by science. The truth is that if God really created the universe, animals, and mankind like He said in Genesis, we should be able to investigate this world and find evidence that what He says is true… and we do!

Think about the difference between the Christian and evolutionary worldviews. If evolution is true, then there is no God and we are the product of random evolutionary processes. As nothing more than a bunch of molecules, we have no purpose in life. On the other hand, if we were created, it means that we were made especially by a loving Creator who has a unique purpose for each of our lives! This difference can completely change a person's life! Truly knowing that God's Word is true is a foundation that will change every aspect of a child's life. That's what we hope to accomplish with the Jonathan Park project – to teach families about scientific evidence that is in harmony with God's Word.

We've designed the audio adventures so families can enjoy them in their cars – while on trips or just running errands. They can listen at home or during family devotional time. Our goal is to provide exciting adventures that run deep with creation apologetics and Biblical lessons. We hope that you enjoy them regardless of where you listen to them!

This Jonathan Park Study Guide has been designed to maximize teaching from each episode in the Jonathan Park Series. Our hope is that after listening to each Jonathan Park Audio Adventure, parents will sit down with their children and work through the information provided in this booklet. Here's how we recommend you use this guide with your child:

1. Listen to an episode from the Jonathan Park: The Adventure Begins – Album #1.
2. Begin your study by praying with your child. Pray that God will teach you truth and continue to build your faith.
3. In the Table of Contents, we've listed Scripture references for each episode. Spend time reading through this section of God's Word.
4. Next, open this Study Guide to the corresponding section. The information is arranged in bite-sized nuggets – each builds upon the previous one. Read through the information with your child and relate it back to the Word of God.
5. Let the child ask questions, and help them find answers. This Study Guide may be the key to unlocking doubts that a child has. Always follow up a child's question. Refer to other creation science resources, or make a commitment to search for the answer together. These questions are excellent ways to take them deeper into God's Word.
6. End in prayer. Thank the Lord for the specific things He has taught during this time.

"But sanctify the Lord God in your hearts: and be ready always to give an answer to every man that asketh you a reason of the hope that is in you with meekness and fear." - I Peter 3:15

How Old is the Earth?

Bible Chronologies

In the Bible, we find many lists which include the names of people and how long those people lived. The lists are known as chronologies. If we add up the people's ages, we can figure out how much time has gone by since Adam and Eve were first created. As it turns out, it seems that the earth is somewhere between about six thousand to ten thousand years old.

Why is the age of the earth so important?

Evolution says that everything has come about by random chance. Since that is impossible, evolutionists try to fix it by saying that over millions of years almost anything can happen. In their minds, the more time evolution has had, the more likely things can develop (or evolve) by random chance. For that reason, evolutionary theory says that the earth is actually billions of years old, instead of the thousands of years that the Bible indicates.

Which viewpoint is right?

If God is the One who actually made the world, then He knows the truth; and He has told us about creation in His Word. How exciting it is to know that science confirms that the Bible is right about the age of the earth!

Days of the Creation Week

Many Christians do not understand the importance of the age of the earth. Unfortunately, they believe evolutionary claims that the earth is billions of years old. Now, those Christians have a problem (or so they think!). How do they equate the Creation account with an evolutionary old earth? Well, instead of sticking to God's truth, they try to squeeze the eternal truths of the all-knowing God into the theories of imperfect humans!

Fitting Millions of Years into the Bible

Since Bible chronologies show Earth to be young, Christians who believe that science has proven Earth to be very old try to fit evolution's millions of years into the days of the creation week. They say that each creation day was a very long period of time, instead of being a twenty-four hour day.

The Old Testament (OT) was originally written in Hebrew. One Hebrew word for "day" is the word "yom." Almost every time, in the hundreds of times it is used in the OT, it means a plain, ordinary, twenty-four hour day. Occasionally the word "yom" can mean a period of time; but in the Genesis creation account, God had the writer always include other words like the first and the second. The Bible also says that it was evening and morning the first day, the second day, and so on. Whenever "yom" is used with the words "first" and "second" or with "evening and morning", it always means a real twenty-four hour day – not a long period of time!

The Bat-lagmite!

In October 1953, National Geographic published a picture of a bat that was stuck in a stalagmite in the Carlsbad Caverns of New Mexico. How did this bat get stuck? How do stalagmites form?

Stalagmite Formation

Stalagmites form when water drops from the ceiling of the cave. Minerals inside the drops stack one on top of another, eventually creating beautiful stalagmites.

Evolutionists claim that this process happens very slowly and, therefore, that stalagmites must take hundreds of thousands of years to form. If that is true, the Bible cannot be right when it indicates that the earth is less than ten thousand years old.

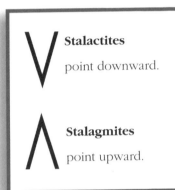

Stalactites point downward.

Stalagmites point upward.

Evolution *vs.* Creation

Could it be that the Book of Genesis is just a story about God using evolution to create? Actually, the order of evolution is completely different from the account in Genesis.

Order of Evolution	Order of Genesis
stars	Earth
our sun	plants
Earth	sun, moon, and stars
mammals	ocean-dwelling animals
flowering plants	land mammals
humans	humans

The Story of the Bat

The bat in the Carlsbad Caverns stalagmite reveals an interesting story. This bat most likely died, fell from the ceiling, and landed right on top of a forming stalagmite. The mineral-filled water kept dropping from the ceiling and minerals began to build up around the bat. The stalagmite grew until it completely encased and fossilized the bat.

Is this evidence that stalagmites form quickly? Yes! If the stalagmite grew too slowly, the bat would have decayed long before the minerals could cover it. Instead, it was covered and fossilized before rotting! The bat's preservation is great proof that stalagmites can form rapidly. However, the preserved bat is not the only proof that stalagmites form rapidly!

More Evidence That Stalactites and Stalagmites Form Quickly

Mollie Kathleen Gold Mine, Cripple Creek, Colorado
After mining stopped in 1961, stalagmites and stalactites began to form. Only forty years later, some of the formations had grown to be nine feet tall and five inches thick.

Sequoyah Caverns, Alabama
Stalagmites have been observed to grow ten inches in ten years.

Jenolan Caves, New South Wales, Australia
In 1954, someone placed a lemonade bottle under a stalactite. Only thirty-three years later, a stalagmite had encased the bottle.

"Six days shall work be done: but the seventh day is the sabbath of rest, an holy convocation; ye shall do no work therein: it is the sabbath of the LORD in all your dwellings." Leviticus 23:3

If you believe the days of creation were millions of years, you would have to say that we are supposed to work six million years and rest one million years. It just does not make sense.

I am tired of working for 6 million years without a break.

The Evidence Shows the World to be Young

We can usually tell the age of a tree by counting rings in its trunk. Trees usually grow one ring a year, though under some conditions the number of rings can vary greatly. Tree rings are physical processes that can help a scientist determine the age of a tree. Likewise, our solar system contains hundreds of physical processes that give clues about the age of our world.

Dr. Russ Humphreys, an ICR physicist, said that if we examine all of the known physical indicators, 90% of them would clearly show the solar system to be much younger than evolutionists claim. Only 10% of those indicators are interpreted to show the earth to be billions of years old. Most of those last 10% get their ages from radioisotopes, which are covered in the next section. A few of these processes are described below:

Shape of Our Galaxy

The shape of our Milky Way Galaxy is a spiral with very distinct arms. Our galaxy is winding itself up. If it were really billions of years old, these arms would already be wound tight and blurred.

Silt on the Ocean Floor

Water and wind erode the continents and deposit materials into the ocean. If the earth were old, a lot more sediment should cover the ocean floor. Also, rivers carry salt into the ocean at a constant rate. If we calculate how long it would take to build up the current amount of salt in the ocean, it is much less than the billions of years taught by evolution.

Comets

Comets constantly circle the sun; and every time they pass by, they lose a part of themselves. In just a few trips around the sun, the comets will burn up and cease to exist. If our solar system is 4.6 billion years old, then why do we still see them? Maybe, it is because the solar system and the comets are much younger than the ages currently given to them.

The Moon

Scientists keeping measurements of the moon's distance from the earth know that it moves away from the earth one centimeter a year. If time could run backward, it would not have been that long ago that the moon's gravitational force would have been strong enough to make it impossible for most things to survive on Earth.

Evidence for the Young Earth

Evidence for a Young Earth from Agriculture and History

5,000 Years Ago
Humans began writing down their history.

10,000 Years Ago
Mankind learned to farm.

90,000 Years without knowledge of farming!

3-8 Million Years Ago
Mankind split off from an ape-like creature.

Evolutionary Tree

Evolutionists believe that mankind and apes split about 3 to 8 million years ago. As cavemen during the "stone age" – 100,000 years ago, mankind was unable to farm. They were strictly hunters and gatherers. Then about 10,000 years ago mankind learned to plant seeds and farm (this claim is based on archeological evidence).

Think about what evolutionists are assuming – that for 90,000 years man did nothing but hunt and gather food from the land! Doesn't it seem more likely that someone would figure out that food could be grown by planting seeds?

Archeology has found many sites which show the intelligence of these "Stone Age" people. For example, they made huge monuments, drew beautiful cave paintings, and kept records of lunar cycles. Why then couldn't man figure out how to farm? The discoveries instead fit very well with the Bible, that man was smart from the start.

Another interesting question is this: when did humans begin to keep track of history? According to evolutionists, it was only 5,000 years ago. Does that seem reasonable? If early man could use his intelligence to make all these wonderful things, why would he wait thousands and thousands of years before recording it?

Biblical *Timeline*

6,000 to 10,000 Years Ago

God creates the earth and mankind, who is smart from the start. Farming begins shortly after creation.

Start of Biblical History

Soon after the creation, mankind begins to record the history of God's people in the Scriptures.

Mid 1800's

Modern mankind begins to believe that he evolved from ape-like creatures.

The Bible is Right

Believing the Bible makes better sense then believing the evolutionary story. The Bible says that God created people not that long ago and that they were intelligent right from the start. If evolutionists believe that farming began only 10,000 years ago and history was written for the first time 5,000 years ago, those dates fit much better with the Bible than they do with evolution.

Although the dates may not be exact, they do show that civilization started suddenly, only a short time ago. That is another great reason to trust in the Bible when it teaches a young age for the earth!

Clams and the Age of the Earth

Thousands of clam fossils, many encased in limestone rock, are found all over the world. Evolutionists say that the limestone layers formed gradually over very long periods of time, but the clams tell us a different story.

How do you normally find clam shells on the beach? They are usually opened up and often lying in halves. After clams die, the muscle holding their two shells together decays and loses its ability to hold the clam tightly shut. The two halves eventually open and usually end up breaking apart.

Why is this evidence that limestone layers form quickly?

Well, first let us talk about the evolutionary explanation for limestone formation. Limestone is made from materials that come from sea animals. According to evolutionists, at one time an ancient sea very slowly deposited limey material, which, over very long periods of time, became a huge limestone layer. During the thousands of years that this layer took to form, clams died, fell to the bottom of the sea, and were, ever so slowly, covered by the limey mud.

What is wrong with this idea? The fact that the fossilized clams are closed! As the clams died, they should have opened up. Remember the muscle connecting the two halves would have decayed and caused the halves to separate from each other. Only pieces and not whole clams would have been covered by the limey mud and eventually become fossilized.

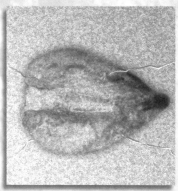

Do you get the point? We find many closed fossilized clams in limestone. The fact that the fossils are closed clams is great evidence that the clams were buried very quickly and so deeply that they could not dig out. The limestone deposit was made so rapidly that the clams did not have time to open up or break into two pieces.

What buried those closed clams with limestone so quickly? The evidence fits perfectly with the worldwide flood of Genesis! The flood's turbulent waters dumped the clams and the limey mud together and the layer solidified to become a limestone rock layer full of fossilized clams. The limestone probably formed very quickly and not over long periods of time. Furthermore, we find massive limestone layers all around the world! Their size is just one more bit of evidence that the Flood occurred just like the Bible describes.

Extra! Extra!

Red Blood Cells Found in Unfossilized T-rex Bone!

In 1990, a team from the Montana State University Museum found an almost complete T-rex skeleton. Later, a team lead by Dr. Mary Schweitzer found red blood cells in the unfossilized long bone of the leg.

Recounting her story in the June 1997 edition of Earth magazine (which has since gone out of business), Dr. Schweitzer said:

When the team brought the dinosaur into the lab, we noticed that some parts deep inside the long bone of the leg had not completely fossilized.

Earlier in the article she reports:

The lab filled with murmurs of amazement, for I had focused on something inside the vessels that none of us had ever noticed before: tiny round objects, translucent red with a dark center.

Then a colleague took one look at them and shouted, "You've got red blood cells. You've got red blood cells!"

Creation Scientists are Excited about Discovery

While evolutionists believe that dinosaurs became extinct almost 65 million years ago, this discovery of red blood cells in a dinosaur bone fits perfectly with the Biblical timeline that indicates that God created all animals only 6,000 to 10,000 years ago. It seems hard to imagine that a bone buried for 65 million years would never have been exposed to the minerals and conditions needed for fossilization to take place. Secondly, since it was not fossilized, how could it stay in the ground for that long without decaying? Even more amazing are the red blood cells. It seems that there is no possible way for something as extremely delicate as red blood cells to survive for 65 million years! This evidence really seems to support the idea that dinosaurs lived thousands of years ago, instead of millions and millions of years ago!

Evolutionary Scientists not Excited about Creation Scientists' Claims

When evolutionists found out that creationists were claiming that this discovery indicates that dinosaurs did not live millions of years ago, they claimed that only heme and not globin (which is needed to form red blood cells) was found in the bones. They said that this distinction was important, because they felt that heme could last millions of years in an unfossilized bone, even if globin could not.

What are Red Blood Cells?

Red blood cells contain a substance called hemoglobin.

This substance contains two ingredients:

1. *Heme* – which is iron.
2. *Globin* – which is a protein.

Testing for Red Blood Cells

Dr. Schweitzer's team became convinced that the T-rex bone contained heme. The big question was whether or not it also contained globin, which would indicate the presence of red blood cells.

To answer the question, scientists under Dr. Schweitzer's direction injected lab rats with the substance from the T-rex bone. If the bone contained only heme, the rats immune system would not react to it. However, if the substance also contained globin, the rats would show a reaction.

What happened? After being injected, the lab rats did have a reaction, showing that both heme and globin were present. That result indicates that Dr. Schweitzer and her team did indeed find hemoglobin, which means red blood cells, in an unfossilized T-rex bone!

Creationists not Satisfied

Even though the evolutionists claim they found only heme in the dinosaur bone, three major problems exist with the idea that this dinosaur lived millions of years ago:

1. How could an unfossilized bone survive unchanged for millions of years?

2. Creation scientists believe that heme absolutely could not survive in that bone for 65 million years, even if it were carefully preserved in a laboratory.

3. Dr. Schweitzer's team originally tested the bone sample for globin and had concluded that there was, in fact, heme and globin present. Both are found in red blood cells.

All of this evidence strongly shows that hemoglobin in this dinosaur bone could not possibly last for 65 million years! This evidence fits perfectly with the Bible when it indicates that Earth is only thousands of years old!

Does Radioisotope Dating Prove that Rocks are Millions of Years Old?

When ask people why they think that the earth is millions of years old, the most common answer is that they believe that rock layers have been proven to be very old. The method most often used for dating rocks is radioisotope dating.

How Does Radioisotope Dating Work?

Imagine filling a glass with ice and then leaving the room for fifteen minutes. When you return, some of the ice will have melted into water.

Now, imagine entering a room and finding a glass of water with just a little sliver of ice left. By comparing the amount of remaining ice to the amount of water, you could guess that the cup had been sitting there long enough for the ice to have melted.

That way of measuring time is very similar to the process used in radioisotope dating. Rocks have radioactive materials that decay into other materials over time.

For instance, in some rocks there is radioactive material known as uranium. Over time, uranium decays into lead. The rate at which uranium decays into lead is believed to be very constant. To find out the age of a rock, you can compare the amount of uranium and lead still present and calculate how long it took for the lead present in the rock to have decayed from uranium.

Uranium/lead is only one of several types of radioisotope dating but the basic method is unchanged. All is well with the radioisotope dating world, right? Wrong! Several assumptions are ignored that make radioisotope dating inaccurate.

Why Does Radioisotope Dating Not Work?

When dating rocks, scientists often make many different unproven assumptions, such as:
• what the rock was originally like,
• whether the rock changes at a constant rate over long periods of time,
• whether there is anything around the rock that would affect the minerals inside it.
Those assumptions make dating rocks nothing more than a guessing game at best.

Mount St. Helens

In case after case, these dating methods have been proven wrong! When Mount St. Helens erupted in May of 1980, it produced brand new rock in its lava dome. When the rock was dated with radioisotope dating, it was measured to be over 2 million years old (but at the time it was less than 20 years old)!

R.A.T.E.

An international team of creation scientists formed a research team to tackle the inaccuracy of radioisotope dating. The name of the project is RATE, which stands for Radioisotopes and the Age of The Earth. These scientists have done cutting-edge research to show why dating rocks produces inaccurate data. Christians do not need to be intimidated when evolutionists say that radioisotope dating has proven rocks to be millions of years old. Actually, the scientific evidence is showing otherwise. It is in harmony with the Bible!

Millions of Years of Death

It is hard for most of us to accept the fact that someday each of us will die. We hate death and so does God. Why then does He allow it? Well, remember, God created things perfect, without death, pain, or suffering. Then God gave Adam a choice: to live the way He wanted us to or to do things his own way. Very sadly, Adam chose the second option – and we have followed in his footsteps, rebelled against God, and chosen to ignore God's ways. Death is in the world because of the wages of our rebellion

"For the wages of sin is death; but the gift of God is eternal life through Jesus Christ our Lord." – Romans 6:23

Believing in Millions of Years Does Not Fit with Romans

Many Christians claim to believe not only this verse from Romans but also something that says exactly the opposite. They want to believe that the earth is very old and that the days of the creation week were not really days but long periods of time. They say that during those long periods of time-----way before God created Adam and Eve—animals, like dinosaurs and others, roamed the earth. They want to believe both evolutionary scientists when they say that the earth is billions of years old and the Bible when it indicates otherwise. That desire gets them into theological trouble. If animals lived and died for millions of years before Adam and Eve were created, then death came into the world long before mankind even had a chance to sin. Death, therefore, could not be a result of Adam's sin. However, death before man cannot be because Romans says:

"Wherefore, as by one man sin entered into the world, and death by sin; and so death passed upon all men, for that all have sinned." – Romans 5:12

The Bible makes it very clear that Adam and Eve's sin caused death; it was not already a part of the world when they were created.

Jesus' Death on the Cross

As a matter of fact, the belief that there were millions of years of death before Adam and Eve wipes out the reason for Jesus dying on the cross. Think about it! If death existed before Adam sinned, then death is normal. It could not really be the penalty for sin. If it is not the penalty for sin, what did the death of Jesus accomplish? Did He really pay the penalty for our sin? Believing in the millions of years takes away the very reason Jesus died on the cross. As it is, God calls us to come to know Him so we can spend an eternity with Him and be free from the horrible effects of sin.

"O death, where is thy sting? O grave, where is thy victory? The sting of death is sin; and the strength of sin is the law. But thanks be to God, which giveth us the victory through our Lord Jesus Christ."

I Corinthians 15:55-57

> *"For the invisible things of him from the creation of the world are clearly seen, being understood by the things that are made, even his eternal power and Godhead; so that they are without excuse."* Romans 1:20

Romans 1:18-32 explains a process of what happens when God is no longer recognized as Creator. Read the passage in your Bible and see what happens:

1. God as creator is denied
2. They did not glorify and were not thankful
3. Their thoughts were futile and hearts darkened

4. They worshiped the creation
5. They lived a lifestyle of sin

When God is taken out of your foundations, your thinking and behavior change. Eventually sin becomes a way of life. But when God is King of your life the process is very different:

1. Practice recognizing God as creator
2. Be thankful and give God honor
3. Take every thought captive; think on what is true right pure…
4. Worship God the creator
5. You will be guided to a holy life through obedience.

It is important that you really know that God is creator because that understanding affects all aspects of your life.

Let's practice together recognizing God as creator. Look at the ordinary scene below. Notice the woodpecker, tree, sky, horse, bat, and the water cycle. We will be looking at the amazing design of each of these created things and recognize and give God glory for his creation.

Willy the Woodpecker

Willy's Tongue

The woodpecker has an incredible tongue connected to cartilage and bones that wrap around its head under the skin. This gives the bird a place to put its long tongue structure.

Willy's Feet

Most birds have "perching feet" with three toes pointing forward and one toe pointing back so that they can grip branches. Woodpeckers' feet are different - they have two toes facing forward and two facing back. This helps them to firmly grip tree trunks so they can hold on while they peck about 15 times a second! If they had regular bird feet, they would not be able to land onto tree trunks, and certainly would not be able to hold on against the forces of their own pecks. Their unusually stiff tail feathers press against the tree trunks to help them balance and climb.

Design in Trees

Trees and plants have fancy systems for moving the food and water that they need around. They get most of the water they need up from their roots to the stems and leaves.

It's a One-way Street

God equipped trees with a special system to move the water from the roots up and from the leaves down. The transport system is made up of cells called xylem (zy-lem) and phloem (flow-em). Xylem are one-way tubes that carry water and minerals upward, like cars moving through tunnels. Phloem are tubes that carry sugar made in the leaves down to other parts of the tree.

Activity
Materials:

Tall stalk of celery   Glass of water   Blue food coloring

What is an intermediate?

Evolution usually explains animals evolving as a slow process. In order for an animal to get to its present way of looking, it had to go through several changes. Evolutionary scientists are looking for animal fossils that show a transition from one type of animal to another kind. One example is how they are looking for a reptile whose scales are becoming feathers. If they found it would be called an "intermediate" between a reptile and a bird. This "intermediate" animal would show evolutionary change happening, BUT it has never been found!

Imagine what the supposed "intermediate" woodpecker would have been like.

I should've evolved a harder beak, the shock absorbing tissue... etc. Now, I am hungry.

- What if a bird had the long tongue of the woodpecker, but lacked the supporting structures (the cartilage, muscles and bones) to pull it back into its head? Would it then fly around with its tongue hanging out?
- What if the bird had not evolved the shock absorbing tissues in its skull? Would its brains rattle around when it pecked on trees?
- What if its toes were not facing the right direction to hold onto tree trunks? It would slip off when it hit the trunk!
- What if it evolved all the right parts, except it had a soft beak? It would take one peck and its beak would fold up!

We recognize God as Creator!

The woodpecker is a good example to us that a wise God created the world, because it has all the necessary parts to work together to make this bird to do what it does!

Just as the woodpecker is designed, the trees that it depends on also show design.

Procedure:

Take a stalk of celery and soak it in a glass of water. Add enough food coloring to turn the water blue. You will see the coloring move gradually up the stalk. You can even cut the stalk part way and soak the two ends in different colors! This shows the xylem water transport cells in the celery.

Chloroplasts

A Large Stack of Pancakes

What does a stack of pancakes and photosynthesis have in common? Inside the cells of a leaf are parts called *chloroplasts* -- and inside these chloroplasts are stacks of pancakes!! No not really! They just look like pancakes. The stacks of pancakes are called *thylakoids*. Inside the chloroplasts is where plants turn light into sugar. This is called photosynthesis.

Thylakoids

The tree takes in carbon dioxide from the air, and this mixes with the sunlight. Through several chemical reactions food and sugar is made for the tree. Leaves are usually flat so that they can get as much light as possible. Maybe that's why the "stacks of pancakes" inside the cells are also flat!

Sun Moon and Stars

As part of our picture at the beginning of the lesson, the sun moon and stars show God's design and play an important part in the design of the universe.

"The heavens declare the glory of God; And the firmament shows His handiwork." Psalm 19:1

As we recognize and glorify God we are joining in with all of creation declaring His glory.

The sun provides light making 'day'. This light is energy that the earth is dependant upon-like leaves dependant on light for photosynthesis. Our sun is a star-all stars are suns. A scientist named Donald DeYoung says "if the sun could be hollowed out like a giant pumpkin, a million planet earths could easily fit inside". THAT'S A BIG SUN!

The stars are signs for different seasons and have served many purposes through the centuries from navigation for boats to exploration, as well as seeing the greatness of our God.

There are more than 10,000,000,000,000,000,000,000 stars -- and each is unique. On a clear night you can see about 3,000 stars with your naked eye. The North Star, called Polaris, is a unique star because from earth it does not appear to move like the rest of the stars which move across the sky from East to West. It does not look like it moves because it is almost directly over the earth's North Pole.

Locating the North Star
First find the Big Dipper constellation. Locate the two end stars of the cup, they Point to the North Star.

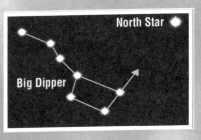

The moon is the perfect light to rule the night. The moon has no light of its own. It just reflects the sun's light to the earth. Just as we are supposed to reflect Christ's light to the world.

The moon interacts with the earth in many ways. One of these ways is through gravity. The moon causes the oceans tides and helps with the earths 23 fi degree tilt, which in turn causes the earth's seasons.

We only see one side of the moon. This is because the moon rotates during the same time period that it also orbits around the earth-about 29 fi days. This keeps only one side facing the earth.

To see this effect tie a string around a tennis ball and swing it around your head. If your head is the earth, the tied side of the ball is always facing you.

Horses

Have you ever wondered how horses can sleep standing up?

They are designed to be able to sleep standing up. Their ligaments and muscles are designed to hold up all that weight without exerting any effort. That's quite a feat when you think about the fact that the average horse may weigh 1,200 pounds!

Another amazing feature about the horse is its hoof. It is made out of tiny, hair-like tubules. They're arranged in a feather-like pattern in such a way that it relieves the pressure on the hoof from hundreds of pounds per square inch, to about four ounces per square inch. This amazing hoof also contains a shock-absorbing cushion called a *Digital Cushion*.

Since the horse has long legs, it makes it difficult for circulation to get the blood back up the legs. So God has designed the hoof with a pump! Every time the horse takes a step, it compresses this pump and helps move the blood back up the legs.

Horses and Evolution

Many museum displays and school textbooks show fossil horse evolution as one of the best supports for evolution. They usually display a "series" showing the horse evolving over time.

An evolutionary "series" shows a group of plants or animals, as seen in the fossil record, supposedly evolving from simple to complex.

A "series" is a number of similar things coming one after another. The World Series, for example in baseball, is a series of baseball games played in a row. An evolutionary series means that similar fossil animals are found one after the other in the layers of the earth.

Simple to complex refers to the anatomy of the plant or animal found as a fossil. Whether a fossil is simple or complex refers to its size, shape, and inner workings of the animal.

Observe the following shapes

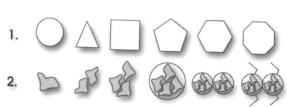

Do you see a pattern?
What is the pattern in the first series of shapes?
What is the pattern in the second series of shapes?

The patterns illustrate a shape going from simple to complex. This is similar to looking at whether a fossil series is going from simple to complex.

To be a good example and support for evolution, such series need to pass two tests:

Test 1 - The shapes of the fossil animals is the series should go from simple to complex.

Test 2 - The simple animals should be in a lower layer of rock than the complex animal. This means that the age of the fossils would go from old, at the bottom layer, to young at the upper layers.

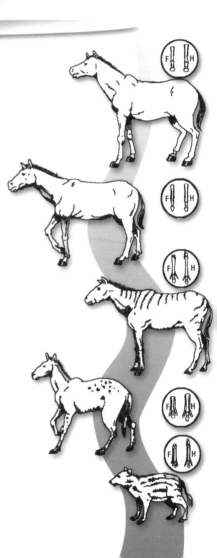

According to evolutionists, the horse series goes as follows.

Equus - the modern horse large with one in size, toe front and back and grazing type teeth.

Then was Pliohippus - the size of a pony, three-toed, and a grazer, and a longer snout.

Next one down is Merychippus, which also had three toes, but had grazing teeth.

Mesohippus, evolved from Eohippus which was slightly larger, had three toes on the front, and was also a browser.

The badger-like Eohippus had four toes on the front feet and three on the rear, was the size of a badger, had browsing teeth, and a short snout.

Test 1 - Does the anatomy of the animals go from simple to complex?

In some ways, it does. Size does change from small to larger, and the toes change from 4 toes in the front to 1. Except that three-toed and one-toed have both been found in the SAME layer, and there is NO two-toed fossil!?

 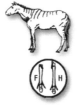 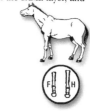

That, however, is not the entire picture…

Look at the ribs: The numbers of ribs in these fossil animals do not go in an order that would show an increase in complexity. Notice that the oldest fossil horse has the same number of ribs as the youngest fossil horse.

18 ribs	15 ribs	19 ribs	18 ribs
Eohippus	Orohippus (Not pictured)	Pliohippus	Equus

Look at the size: The size range of horses that live today can go from 18 inches all the way to 6 1/2 feet! So size really isn't a result of evolution either.

The fossil series failed to pass Test 1. What we do see are some similarities in different animals. This is proof of horses evolving.

Test 2 - Are the animals in the correct order?

Are these animals really found in the correct order in the fossil record? Is Eohippus in the older (lower) layers and are the others in younger (upper) rock layers? In some places, yes they are.

 But in South America, the fossil evidence is very different. One-toed fossil animals that are very similar to the modern horse, lie in layers LOWER than animals with three toes!

If interpreted in the evolutionary manner, the one-toed horses should have evolved into three-toed horses. And also, in Oregon and Nebraska, fossils of three-toed and one-toed horses are found together in the same layer.

The fossil horse series fails to pass Test 2 as well!

How do creationists interpret this?

Creationists think that these fossil animals all lived at the same time, and their fossils were deposited during the flood. It is likely that most of these fossil animals could be grouped into three separate created "kinds" of animals - all created on the 6th day of the creation week.

Bats

Bats are incredible creatures! Instead of being guided by their eyesight, insect-eating bats hunt with their ears!

If made to fly in a pitch-black room with fine wires suspended from ceiling to floor, these bats would rarely ever hit a wire as they flew around the room.

In the wild, these night hunters find small insects. One small brown bat can catch 600 mosquitoes per hour. Do you know how bats can do this?

Echolocation of Bats

They have a special voice box that sends out very high-pitched sounds. If something like a bug, a tree, or another bat is in the area, the sound wave bounces off of it.

The process of bat hearing:

The bat's special large ears hear the super-high pitched squeaks and echoes bouncing back from the trees and bugs. The echo sends a message to the bat's brain to be interpreted. The brain helps the bat tell the difference between its own sounds, from those of other bats, and from what location the sound bounces back from. The bat then calls in that same direction in order to hear if the object is moving and to tell where it located.

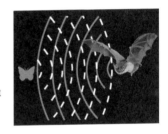

Using this same method, the bat can also determine the size, speed, direction, and surface texture of its prey! Its little brain understands this all in just moments as it is flying around! The bat's ability to hunt using sounds and echoes is called "echolocation." Do you know of another animal that uses echolocation? The Dolphin!

Wait a Minute…Time Out!!

Let's explain again a few things about how evolution is supposed to work.
Just in case you don't understand. Let's start at the beginning.

and so on...

Amoeba   multi-celled   fish   amphibian   reptile

According to evolution, the first life was a one celled creature like an amoeba. That it slowly became a multi-celled creature. The multi-celled creature then became the first fish. Through many more changes, the fish grew one leg from its fin, then another, then another and so on until the fish had four legs and now would be called an amphibian. The fish with one, two, or three legs is called an *intermediate* between a fish an amphibian because it is changing from a fish into an amphibian. *This intermediate animal does not exist in real life or in the fossil record*, it is just an idea, just an artist's drawing. In order for evolution to happen, the intermediate animal has to evolve something that gives that animal an advantage -- it has to be better. For example, a fish growing legs has to be better than just having fins.

You decide, would it be better for a fish to have three fins and one leg or all four fins? Why or Why not?

Okay- Let's continue with Bats

For evolution of bat echolocation to occur, the bat had to evolve three things separately at different times.

It needs the special voice box.
It needs the very sensitive ears.
It needs the brain to understand the signals of echolocation.

If each of these parts evolved slowly over time the bat would die before all the parts were finally able to work together. The intermediate bat would just have a voice box but his ears could not hear the sound and its brain could not understand it. *The bat must have all three of these parts working together, fully functioning, to find its food, know its surroundings, and find other members of its family.*

Let's talk a little bit about what it means to be a fully functioning bat.
Take a model airplane for example. At the store you can by a model of an airplane that you can put together.

First, we have all the parts.

The airplane can not function because it is just in parts.

Second we must put the parts together.

Is this an airplane? The person putting it together must know how to make the airplane correctly or it will not work.

Third, we must read the directions to put together a fully functioning plane.

All the parts are in the right places-the plane can function.

Conclusions about fully functional airplanes and bats:

The person putting together the plane must have a plan and know what the final plane should look like. Just like how God has made all things already put together-No assembly is required. A bat was made with its parts fully functioning so that it could live and grow.

The Evidence - Fossil bats:

The evidence from the fossil record shows that bats have always had the echolocation ability! The fossil bats that we have actually found are supposed to be 50 million years old. Yet they look about the same as bats do today, and they have the same echolocation system. This evidence definitely fits with the creation model that God created things fully put together. The fossil record provides no evidence that bats evolved their abilities!

What's the point?

Remember what we are doing? Studying and acknowledging God as the creator!

Bats, though they may be so ugly that they are cute, show that an intelligent designer had to be planning out every part of a bat.

Look back at the picture that is at the beginning of this episode. There is one item left to talk about. Can you see what it is? Most of us take for granted what is called the water cycle. It does its important job behind the scenes!

The Water Cycle

Why is water so important?

The Earth is the only planet known to have large bodies of liquid water. Over 70% of the surface of the earth is covered in water!

Properties of Water

The water on our planet is an essential part of keeping earth suitable for life. Water keeps the temperature on Earth moderate.

A property of water is that it absorbs lots of heat energy very quickly without changing its temperature. So during the day, the water bodies absorb heat from the sun and keep the earth cooler. Then at night, they give off heat and prevent the earth from getting too cold. Without the oceans on our planet, some areas on land would get hot enough to boil water in the day and then freezing cold at night.

The design of the water molecule attracts and repels certain things.

Water loving

Things that stick to water are called hydrophilic. These things easily dissolve in water, such as sugar.

Water dreading (Fear of water)

Things that do not stick to water are called hydrophobic. These things do not dissolve in water, such as oil.

Oil does not dissolve in water it would rather stick to itself than to the water. Oil is called a hydrophobic substance.

Water can be stretched with out the surface being broken. This is called *cohesion*. An example of this is a bug resting on the surface without falling into the water. Water molecules like each other and so they tend to stay together. So the water has a surface in which bugs and leaves can rest.

Some things can easily dissolve in water. When they do, it's called a solvent. This is important because our bodies, plants and animals depend on nutrients, mineral, and chemicals that can dissolve in water.

Our oceans also act as holding tanks for certain chemicals. For example, carbon dioxide dissolves in water. So the oceans keep the amount of carbon dioxide in the air in balance. When more is created, like when we burn fossil fuels (gas and oil), the excess is stored in the ocean and the amount in the atmosphere changes very little.

An interesting property of water is that is shrinks when it is cooled until it begins to freeze and then it expands-gets bigger. This causes ice to float!!

This is of importance because it prevents the oceans from freezing from bottom to top. If it did not expand, the ice would be most heavy and would sink to the bottom. Since it does expand, it stays near the surface and floats.

Water that is warmer than 4 degrees C is heavier and sinks to the bottom, warming the bottom of the ocean or lake. This movement of water from top to bottom, together with the wind patterns, produces some of the ocean currents.

Percipitation

Evaporation

Run-off water flow

The Cycle

Water is naturally recycled throughout the earth. Follow the arrows to see where the water travels on the earth.

 Evaporation is when water molecules escape into the air:
- Water evaporates from the oceans forming clouds.
- Water evaporates from plants and the land forming clouds.

 Precipitation is rainfall that returns to earth:
- Rain falls over the ocean from clouds.
- Rain falls over the land from clouds.

Surface and ground water flow:

Water flows into lakes and rivers as it drains from the land after it has rained. This water eventually makes it to the ocean. Water also seeps into underground areas and then drains back into the ocean.

The Process:

The sun causes water to evaporate from the ocean, lakes, and streams forming water vapor. The vapor clumps together forming clouds -droplets of water. The clouds move over the land. Rain falls from the clouds onto the land. This rain then drains its way through lakes, rivers, and underground systems back into the ocean. Every ecosystem of the earth depends on this cycle for water and nutrients to sustain life!!

Water really has a huge impact on our planet, and without it, life as we know it could not exist!

Did you know that raindrops are the perfect size? If they were bigger they would cause damage and if they were smaller they would disappear before even hitting the earth.

Summary

Like Romans 1:18 says, God's creativity is seen all around us. Let's give Him praise for His incredible majesty!

Bible Lesson

Romans 12:17 "*Recompense to no man evil for evil. Provide things honest in the sight of all men.*"

1Peter 3:3 & 9 "*Finally, be ye all of one mind. Having compassion one of another, love as brethren, be pitiful, be courteous: not rendering evil for evil, or railing for railing: but contrariwise blessing; knowing that ye are thereunto called, that ye should inherit a blessing.*"

When strangers or friends offend you or wrong you it is hard to have a soft heart towards them, but when you harden your heart towards others, you also harden your heart toward God loving you in that same place. It's often hard to follow God when you rely solely upon your feelings. When you are offended or hurt repeatedly we often want to get back at them. Your feelings are real, but they may not always be right feelings. This means that you do not need to deny that you feel a certain way, but realize that you to need to choose God's way. This is hard to do, but it is what the Creator asks of us. God often uses hard situations to grow you into a person with honor and character.

God also deserves acknowledgment for creating humans-every type of human no matter if they are stranger, friend, or enemy. God loves and has compassion on all people. Praise be unto Him!

The Evolutionary Tree

Have you ever seen the evolutionary tree? This diagram is used by evolutionists to try and figure out what animals evolved from other animals.

At the base of the tree, is the single cell. Then as the tree branches upward, animals become more and more complex. As you move further up the tree, some groups of animals become so different from each other that they begin a new branch on the tree.

At each split, there is a common ancestor that leads to the next group of animals that share similar traits.

This evolutionary tree is how evolutionists try to explain the order in which all animals, plants, and humans evolved. The ***assumption*** is that animals with similar characteristics evolved from common ancestors *(they shared the same parents and grandparents)*.

Convergent Evolution

Unfortunately, the evolutionary tree doesn't fit together as well as they would like. The problem is this: **there are many examples of animals that are so different that evolutionists have put them on opposite sides of the evolutionary tree, and yet they share a very similar trait**.

So how do evolutionists explain two animals that supposedly evolved completely separately from each other, yet share similar characteristics? Well, since in their mind these animals evolved completely separately from each other, they believe these traits evolved two different times -- by accident! This theory is what is known as *convergent evolution*.

Evolutionary Tree

The Wolf

Tasmanian Wolf

Carried their young in a pouch just like a kangaroo.

Timber Wolf

Gives birth like all other mammals.

The Tasmanian wolf has been given the scientific name of *Thylacinus cnocephalus* which means "pouched dog". This amazing creature had a pouch like a kangaroo in which they carried their young. Animals with a pouch like this are known as **marsupials**. Unfortunately the last captive Tasmanian wolf died in 1936 at the Hobart Zoo in Hobart, Tasmania in Australia.

On the evolutionary tree, marsupials and mammals that give live child birth are on completely separate branches. Because they give birth is so different, evolutionists claim they do not share a close common ancestor. That means evolution had to accidentally make two different wolves that look very similar.

Now we can see silliness of this idea of convergent evolution. The odds that random, accidental mistakes could form *one* wolf are **impossible**! To say that random, accidental mistakes could make a wolf two completely different times would be… **Impossible x 2!**

Flight

When we think of animals that fly, birds are usually the first thing that comes to mind. However, there are many other types of creatures that can fly. In the space below, see if you can make a list of animals that fly:

With a little effort, you can make a pretty long list of flying animals. Some of those animals on your list were probably similar, but some were most likely very different from each other. As a matter of fact there are some animals that can fly that are so different from each other, that evolutionists say they had to evolve completely separately from each other - they're not even close on the evolutionary tree! So as a result, they believe that the miracle of flight had to evolve at least 4 separate times:

1. Bird flight   2. Insect flight   3. Mammal Flight   4. Reptile Flight

Now go back to your list and place a (**B**), (**I**), (**M**), or (**R**) for **B**ird, **I**nsect, **M**ammal, or **R**eptile flight next to each animal on your list. Did you come up with an animal in each of the four categories? The easiest were probably birds and insects. If you didn't list any for mammals or reptiles, here's one for each:

Mammals: Bats; Reptiles: Pterosaurs

The Miracle of Flying

We often take flying for granted in our modern day, but what an amazing miracle! Flying is such a complex thing that mankind couldn't even figure out how to do it until fairly recently. The Wright Brothers first took to the air in 1903.

However, long before man figured it out, the Creator had already made incredible designs we'll never be able to copy! Consider how creative He was when He made the birds:

- Their feathers are strong and lightweight.
- They have powerful, perfectly designed wing muscles.
- Their bones are hollow so they are light, and yet flexible for flying.

We could write an entire book about how perfectly the bird was designed for flying. If each one of these characteristics were not perfectly designed, there would be no way that a bird could ever get off the ground.

Now consider how impossible it would be for these precisely designed animals to be made by the evolutionary process of random accidents!

The problem gets worse for evolutionists. Just as *bird* flight is a miracle, so is insect, mammal, and reptile flight. Each of these groups is so different from each other, that evolutionists say that they cannot be related. However, they all have the miracle of flight.

According to convergent evolution, this miracle of flight not only evolved once, but had to evolve four different times!

Which of the following animals has an eye that is the most similar to humans?

a). Flies   **b). Snails**   **c). Squid**   **d). Bee**   **e.) Worm**

Believe it or not, if you chose *squid*, you're right! The squid eye is similar to ours in the way it focuses with a lens, and because of the muscles that rotate the eye.

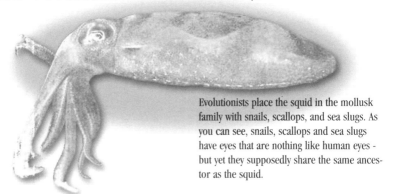

Evolutionists place the squid in the mollusk family with snails, scallops, and sea slugs. As you can see, snails, scallops and sea slugs have eyes that are nothing like human eyes - but yet they supposedly share the same ancestor as the squid.

So how do evolutionists explain that the squid evolved an eye similar to humans from an ancestor that has completely different eyes? They say it was random mutations!

However, both the squid eye and the human eye are such extremely complex and delicate systems for sight. There's no way that random, accidental mistakes could design something so similar... twice!

Antifreeze Fish

According to evolutionists, there was a group of fish that split in two groups about 40 million years ago. One group now called *Antarctic Notothenioid* went to Antarctica and the other, now known as *Northern Cod*, went to the Artic on the other side of the world. At this time they supposedly began evolving separately from each other.

Antarctic Notothenioid

Northern Cod

Then about 25 million years ago, according to evolutionary theory, these two poles of the earth began to freeze. Each of these two groups of fish would have frozen, but they evolved an "antifreeze" that kept them alive:

- They have special elements in their blood called glycoprotein.
- This glycoprotein keeps their blood from freezing - kind of like antifreeze in a car.

The **protein** that makes this antifreeze is so different in each of the two groups of fish, that it confirmed evolutionists' belief that these two fish evolved completely independently of each other.

Now here's the amazing thing. The antifreeze from both groups of fish is almost identical. How could two groups of fish, who began evolving completely independent from each other, develop similar antifreeze that is produced by a totally different gene? There is no way that this could be possible!

A better explanation is the Creator made both the fish, and the antifreeze!

Other Examples of Convergent Evolution

In *Jonathan Park & the Mysterious Stranger*, Nick Williams builds an oak display for the museum. Look at his display to learn about other examples of supposed convergent evolution:

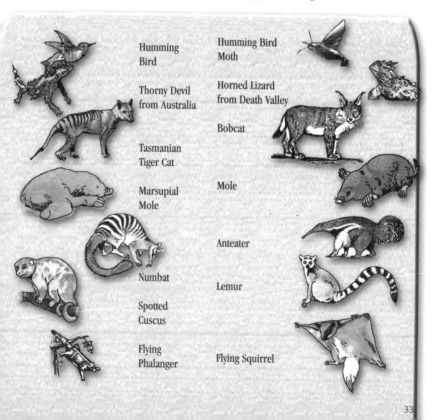

Humming Bird   Humming Bird Moth

Thorny Devil from Australia   Horned Lizard from Death Valley

Tasmanian Tiger Cat   Bobcat

Marsupial Mole   Mole

Numbat   Anteater

Spotted Cuscus   Lemur

Flying Phalanger   Flying Squirrel

There Are Two Ways to Explain Common Traits in Unrelated Animals:

Evolution

Common traits point to a common evolutionary ancestor.

But in the case of convergent evolution, this idea is totally destroyed.

Creation

Common traits point to a common designer.

Even human engineers use designs they like in many different ways. It makes sense that God would use similar designs in completely different animals -- they live in similar environments, breath the same air, eat some of the same food, etc.

So when we see common characteristics, it points to design by a Creator, not convergent evolution - and that's what the Bible's been saying all along!

Showing Kindness

In *Jonathan Park & the Mysterious Stranger* the Brenan family took in Nick Williams. They give him a job and let him stay in their barn. The Bible says that we need to act out our faith, not just talk about it. In other words, if we know God loved the world by sending His Son to die for them, then we need to show the world God's love.

THE FIRST BOOK
OF MOSES,
CALLED
GENESIS.

"If a brother or sister be naked, and destitute of daily food, And one of you say unto them, Depart in peace, be ye warmed and filled; notwithstanding ye give them not those things which are needful to the body; what doth it profit?" -James 2:15, 16.

The root word "thermo" means heat, and "dynamics" means power. So thermodynamics is the study of heat-power. Thermodynamics is all about how energy behaves.

Heat is often called a form of energy. Sunlight is heat energy. You can feel the energy from the sun as it warms your body.

Energy can be defined as the ability to do work.

Work is a force that causes movement. For example, you have to do work to clean your room.

Scientists have determined that there are certain ways that energy behaves. These ways have been called laws because they are stable and do not change. Although we now know of three laws of thermodynamics, we want to talk about two of them:

THE LAWS OF ENERGY

1st Law of Thermodynamics – Law of Conservation of Matter:

Matter is a fancy word for objects or things. This law says that no new energy or matter is being made and none is being destroyed—it is just changing form. Energy made from flowing water and a hydroelectric dam is not new energy. The energy is already present in the moving water, and is then captured by the turbines in the dam and changed into electricity, a different form of energy.

Have your parents or teachers ever said things like:

"Turn off the lights so we *conserve* electricity"

"During a drought it is important to *conserve* water"

To *conserve* means to save. The above law states that energy is conserved, meaning that although energy is used, it is not lost, but simply changes into a different *form* of energy.

What is meant by the word "form"?
A "form" is a different type of the same thing. For example, Water has three "forms."

It is still water,
just a different "form".

Liquid—water　　**Gas—steam**　　**Solid—ice**

This is also the way it is with energy. Energy and matter are not lost when they are used. They just become a different type of energy or matter. Like sunlight captured by the leaves of a plant, it changes to a different form. When it is in a plant, it is no longer sunlight energy, but what is called chemical energy.

'Form' A	becomes	'Form' B
Sunlight energy	··············	Chemical energy
Coal as fuel for a train	··········	Steam
Gasoline	·····················	Moving car
Wind	·······················	Electricity

How does Form A become Form B? There is a plan that changes the energy from one type into another type. Gas is put into a car engine. Wind energy is captured by a windmill and changed into electricity.

The 1st Law Opposes the Theory of Evolution

This law of science tells us that no new energy can ever be made or destroyed. However, our universe is filled with tons and tons of energy. If no new energy can be created, where did it all come from in the first place? Evolution has no answer for this question, but the Bible does! It tells us that God created all things from the beginning – including energy.

2nd Law of Thermodynamics – Law of Increased Entropy:

Entropy is just a fancy word for disorder. Things are constantly getting more disorderly when left to themselves. Deterioration, decay, and disorder are words that all describe the same process of falling apart, like a piece of fruit that has been left on the counter and begins to decay and rot.

Let's observe with our senses the 2nd law of thermodynamics:

What can you observe about a car when it just sits for years in a driveway?

What can you observe about your bedroom over time?

What can you observe about your own body over time?

The following story illustrates the 2nd law of thermodynamics:

Suzy inherited her grandmother's beautiful garden. In it were lilacs, rhododendrons, roses, columbines, a pond with a fountain, and a few fish. She was busy working at the office and did not have time to visit the garden for several months. When she finally went to the garden, she could hardly see the flowers. The place was overgrown with grass and a vine called Deadly Nightshade, and boy was it deadly. Besides being poisonous, it had wrapped its viney arms all over her grandmother's flowers and was beginning to choke them out. It was very unruly and disorderly. She thought to herself, "Wow the 2nd law of thermodynamics is at work here in the garden. I had better invest some energy into restoring order or it will continue to be a mess of random weeds."

In this small garden system, it is easy to see that when left to itself, a garden becomes disorderly, and vines and overgrowth replace the original garden order. This is a simple example of the 2nd law of thermodynamics.

The 2nd Law Opposes the Theory of

Evolution says that things have come about and built themselves up into higher more complex levels by natural processes.

Evolution also claims to be a principle of increasing order and newness.

Contradiction: The 2nd Law (which has no known exceptions) is a principle of decay and disorder and evolution is a principle of development and order. Evolution and the 2nd Law disagree with each other.

Can you see how the law of science is opposite of the theory of evolution?

If you were to make this into a graph: One line goes up and one line goes down.

Important Fact: These two laws of thermodynamics always work and have no known exceptions.

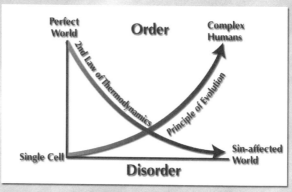

How are the laws of thermodynamics related to your faith in the God of the Bible? Together these two laws of science contradict evolutionary thought.

The 2nd Law of Thermodynamics Can Be Temporarily Reversed

Thermo-Girl Overcomes The 2nd Law

How can the 2nd law be temporarily overcome? The answer is by investing some energy. Think about how your bedroom begins to become disorderly over time. That's the 2nd Law. However, you can temporarily overcome disorder by investing some energy to clean up your room and restore order.

Invest some energy to restore order by:
-working to put you socks in your drawer.
-working to put your dirty clothes in the hamper.
-working to vacuum your carpet.

CLOSED OR OPEN?

So how do evolutionists try to get around the 2nd law of thermodynamics? They say that since we can overcome the 2nd law temporarily -- then maybe a source of energy has allowed evolution to overcome the 2nd Law. But how would energy get to earth? To find out the answer, we need to know the difference between open and closed systems. What does that mean?

The 2nd Law of Thermodynamics can be seen in what are called *open* and *closed* systems.

Closed   Imagine your room as a *closed* room. The blinds are pulled, the windows are shut, and the door is closed. What takes place in the room if nothing enters or exits the room?

Dust accumulates.

Mold may grow.

Smell develops.

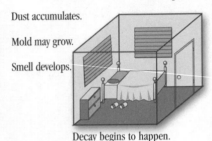

In a closed room it may seem at first that nothing happens, but over time you can observe that things begin to deteriorate. Since no energy can enter a closed system, the 2nd Law cannot be temporarily overcome, so order continues to deteriorate into disorder. This is why most evolutionists would agree that evolution could not happen in a closed system.

Decay begins to happen.

Open   Is the earth an open system? Yes. We receive energy from space and the sun and for this reason, some evolutionists claim that this energy could reverse the 2nd Law on earth, and make evolution possible – but there are two major problems with this idea:

1. The 2nd Law still works in an open system.

Imagine your room as an open room. The blinds and windows are open and the door is open. What takes place if you, your family, the sun, and your dog enter and exit the room?

A mess of dirty clothes develops.
The sun fades and dries things out.
Dust accumulates.
A chewed shoe appears.

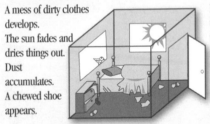

In an open room, it may be easier to see how things can begin to deteriorate because of all the things entering the room. If you are not careful to return everything from the place that it came from or clean up after yourself, the room soon becomes chaotic and disorderly. Is that what your room looks like?

Decay begins to happen.

2. To overcome the 2nd Law, you not only need raw energy, but a plan on how to use the energy.

Creationists argue that energy coming into a system alone actually creates disorder and not new order because there needs to be a way to store and use the new energy that comes into the system.

If a tornado were to strike a junkyard, would it create order or chaos? A tornado is wind energy. What plan is there in a junkyard to store and use the wind energy from a tornado? None.

Think about our example of a room. Lightening is a powerful source of energy. If a lightening bolt struck your room, would it be more orderly? No way!

There may be energy available to make more order but the necessary plan to store and use that energy is missing. Without a plan the result is more disorder. For that reason, evolution is wrong. Even though earth is an open system, the 2nd Law continues to work – and raw energy from space and the sun can't overcome it without an intelligent plan on how to use the energy. That makes evolution impossible – in an open system, or not!

TIME IS TICK'N AWAY

Think of the universe as a wind-up clock.

A wind-up clock has to be 'energized' or wound-up by someone. The winding is giving energy to the clock. That energy is then stored within the clock mechanism and slowly and evenly released in order to make the arms of the clock move and the seconds to tick.

The Steps:

1. Beginning investment of energy. (Someone winding the clock)

2. A plan already in place for the energy to be stored and used. The clock was designed with a spring that tightens -- this is connected through a series of parts and movements that work together to keep time.

3. Eventually the clock has to be wound up again because the available energy was converted into movement.

How is God involved in our universe and the 2nd law?

1. God invested the original energy to create our universe. He in effect "wound up" the universe. Isn't it interesting that our universe and the earth spin in space as if they really were wound up like a spinning top?

2. God designed and created the plan for storage and use of energy. For example, sunlight energy is stored and used in plants and absorbed by the earth.

3. The universe is becoming more disordered ever since mankind rebelled.

4. As promised in the book of Revelation, God will return to restore His creation to perfection, or perfect order.

Together the 1st and 2nd laws of thermodynamics support creation.

Genesis describes a creator investing energy into an original creation. Like a clock being wound up. No energy is now being made (1st law) because "...*on the seventh day God ended his work which he had made; and he rested...*" (Gen. 2:2-3) and is now "...*upholding all things by the word of his power...*" (Heb 1:3)

Genesis 3:17-20 describes sin, death, and decay entering the created world. (2nd law) "...*cursed is the ground for thy sake; in sorrow shalt thou eat of it all the days of thy life; Thorns also and thistles shall it bring forth to thee; and thou shalt eat the herb of the field; In the sweat of thy face shalt thou eat bread, till thou return unto the ground; for out of it wast thou taken: for dust thou art, and unto dust shalt thou return.*"

Conclusion: What do we observe in this world? That the 2nd Law is observable—deterioration and decay " to the dust we shall return." The Bible talks about decay entering the earth. From studying Genesis, we can learn that death first entered the world when Adam and Eve sinned. This is one main place where the 2nd law is seen working in Scripture. **The Bible and the laws of thermodynamics agree with each other.**

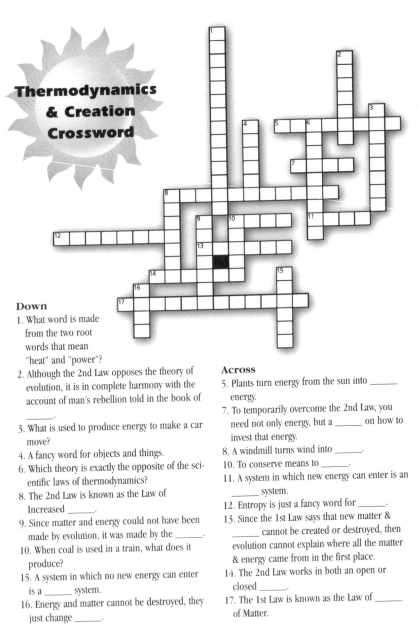

Thermodynamics & Creation Crossword

Down

1. What word is made from the two root words that mean "heat" and "power"?
2. Although the 2nd Law opposes the theory of evolution, it is in complete harmony with the account of man's rebellion told in the book of _____.
3. What is used to produce energy to make a car move?
4. A fancy word for objects and things.
6. Which theory is exactly the opposite of the scientific laws of thermodynamics?
8. The 2nd Law is known as the Law of Increased _____.
9. Since matter and energy could not have been made by evolution, it was made by the _____.
10. When coal is used in a train, what does it produce?
15. A system in which no new energy can enter is a _____ system.
16. Energy and matter cannot be destroyed, they just change _____.

Across

5. Plants turn energy from the sun into _____ energy.
7. To temporarily overcome the 2nd Law, you need not only energy, but a _____ on how to invest that energy.
8. A windmill turns wind into _____.
10. To conserve means to _____.
11. A system in which new energy can enter is an _____ system.
12. Entropy is just a fancy word for _____.
13. Since the 1st Law says that new matter & _____ cannot be created or destroyed, then evolution cannot explain where all the matter & energy came from in the first place.
14. The 2nd Law works in both an open or closed _____.
17. The 1st Law is known as the Law of _____ of Matter.

Sometimes circumstances in our lives seem difficult and unfair. We try, but cannot control the circumstances around us. This could be disheartening unless you can see the larger picture that God is involved in our circumstances and uses them for many purposes—to get our attention, to show us love, to test our integrity, and challenge our choices. His character is good. Have faith in the midst of difficult circumstances by knowing that He will never act outside of His character toward you.

Across: 5. CHEMICAL 7. PLAN 8. ELECTRICITY 10. SAVE 11. OPEN 12. DISORDER 13. ENERGY 14. SYSTEM 17. CONSERVATION
Down: 1. THERMODYNAMIC 2. GENESIS 3. GASOLINE 4. MATTER 6. EVOLUTION 8. ENTROPY 9. CREATOR 10. STEAM 15. CLOSED 16. FORM

40

What is a scientific theory?

A true scientific theory must meet three rules. It must be:

1 Observable   **2** Repeatable   **3** Able to be tested to see if it is true or false.

To explain these three rules let's come up with a theory:

Theory:
Leaves can fall from a tree in three different ways.

Observable
Can you observe our theory with your senses? This means that you use your sight, taste, touch, smell, and hearing to gather information. Some people use computers, test tubes, filters, and instruments to help them do this.

Our theory states that leaves can fall in three different ways. Given that there is no wind, I do observe that there are three main ways leaves fall. The way they fall depends on the shape of the leaf. So our theory is observable.

Repeatable
Can someone else do the same thing and observe the same results that we did? Can they find other tress that will repeat the way that the first tree dropped leaves? Yes they can, so our theory is repeatable.

Able to Be Tested
Can we design an experiment to test our answer to see if it's true or false? Yes, that's because our theory is within our limits of proving true or false. We can do a test to see if we are right.

An unscientific theory would be some thing like, "Leaves on other planets fall in four different ways instead of three." This theory doesn't meet the last rule of being able to be tested to see if it true or false because we've never even found trees on other planets. There is no way to prove this true or false.

However, we can prove our theory to be right. By going from tree to tree and watching leaves fall, we can see if we can only count three different ways that leaves fall. If we found only two or less ways, or four or more ways that leaves fall, our theory would be proven false. Since we see only three patterns that leaves make when they fall, our theory is correct.

Therefore our theory meets the rule of being able to be tested to see if it is true or false.

So our "Falling Leaf Theory" meets the three rules of being a scientific theory!

Now that we know the three rules, which of the following theories is a correct scientific theory?

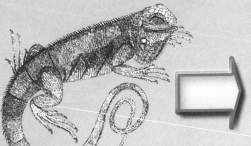

A. A lizard has evolved scales.
B. A lizard has scales.
C. God created lizards with scales.

Statement B is a scientific theory because it can be directly observed and repeated by others, and tested to be true or false. Statements A and C are not valid scientific theories because there is no way of knowing for sure by direct observation and testing.

Theories can become laws when many people have tested them many times. We, for example, test gravity, every moment of every day. When things are dropped, they fall. When I jump, I come back down. If there were no gravity, I would certainly wake up in the morning with "ceiling face" instead of "pillow face" because without gravity I would float to the ceiling.

Are Creation and Evolution true scientific theories?

Put on your thinking cap. (Are they observable, repeatable, and testable?)

Think

Can we directly observe a lizard evolving scales? No!
Can we directly observe God creating lizard scales? No!
Can you think of an experiment?

Evolution - A person could catch a lizard and put it in an aquarium and observe it. How long would you need to wait and observe it in order to know if a lizard was evolving? It would take a very long time. Is this a realistic experiment? No. Can we as humans repeat evolution? No. Can we prove evolution to be true or false? No. Since those who believe in evolution start off by believing that it is true, whenever evidence is presented to show that it is wrong, they simply change the theory to try and fix the problem. So since evolution isn't observable, repeatable, or able to be proven true or false, it is not a true scientific theory.

Creation – If you watched the lizard in its aquarium, could you see it being created? No. That happened in the past. Can we repeat Creation? No. Only God the Creator can do that! Can we prove the Bible true or false simply based on science? No. What if the Biblical account seems to violate a rule of science? Could this disprove the Bible? No. It may be that the Creator stepped outside the limits of our scientific understanding, like parting the Red Sea.

So both evolution and creation are not scientific theories. Does this mean they're both not true?

There are two types of science, which ask different questions.

Origin Science
(What was the beginning?)

Creation and Evolution are called origin sciences. They try to answer the questions, "Where did we come from?" "What was the beginning?" Scientists who study origins try to act out or model situations that may have happened in the past to test if they were possible. Remember that they must act out situations because there were no eyewitnesses(which we can physically talk to) that observed the beginning. These theories are based on ideas about the past, a long time ago.

Operation Science
(How does it work?)

Operation science defines most other types of science. They try to answer the question, "How does it work?" An example is the medical field and the study of diabetes. Some people's bodies do not properly use or make insulin. This is called diabetes. Insulin is needed in the process of changing sugar, starches, and other food into energy. A diabetic can have too much or too little sugar in their blood. If a person has too little sugar in their blood, a glucagon shot can be given to raise the blood sugar level. Scientists' discoveries about this disease and how it works have helped people with diabetes live normal lives.

Can you see the difference between the two types of science?
Origin---What was the beginning? (Not directly observable.)
Operation---How does it work? (Directly observable, repeatable, and testable.)

Crime scene investigators are always looking for trustworthy pieces of evidence to determine how a crime happened. Do you know what makes the best evidence? It would be an eyewitness. An eyewitness is a good piece of evidence because that person has the potential to have seen the details of what took place.

How can so many scientists be mistaken?

They begin with certain ideas of what they think they are going to see. Each person has their own bias in their conclusions.

Coffer Maker Illustration:

Have you ever seen your mother or father make coffee? The Coffee Maker Illustration can help you understand bias.

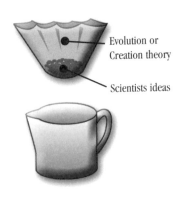

Evolution or
Creation theory

Scientists ideas

The filter and coffee grounds together represent information in your mind. The coffee grounds are ideas. The filter represents a theory (Evolution or Creation). The coffeepot will catch what comes out of the filter.

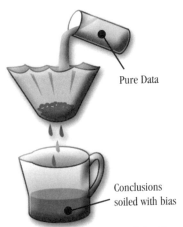

Pure Data

The water being poured into the filter represents pure data or facts. When the water is poured into the filter, it mixes with the grounds. As it seeps through the filter, it is transformed into coffee and comes out into the coffeepot as a dark brown liquid.

Conclusions
soiled with bias

This is like a scientist having a bias. As the data is poured into the filter, it mixes with the ideas of the scientist and the evolution or creation theory. As the data seeps through the filter, it is no longer pure facts; it has been mixed with ideas and theories. The water has been muddied. The dark brown liquid contains bias---it is no longer clear but brown.

What's the point?

This is like a scientist who has bias. When the facts are studied by a scientist, the conclusion is muddied by that person's own thoughts. Bias can cause scientists to make wrong conclusions.

This is why investigating evolution and creation is so difficult; there were no physical eyewitnesses that we can talk to today. We can not travel back in time. So we have to look at the evidence and see which idea – evolution or creation – best fits the evidence.

Were God, Jesus, and the Holy Spirit witnesses to creation? Yes. What source can we look to as a guide for our science? There is God's written Word and the evidence found in the physical world. It all points to a creator.

Religion is a set of beliefs about the universe. Isn't funny that evolution, which is often called a "fact of science", not only doesn't qualify for a valid scientific theory, but fits the definition of religion?

Clarifying questions

When someone is sharing their belief in evolution, there are questions you can ask to help them see that they believe in something -- even though the facts may not agree. These are questions that you can ask politely when your teacher, or anyone else, is discussing evolution. It may be that your questions will help the other students to see that your teacher is talking about religion, not science.

The four questions are:

I. What do you mean by what you are saying? (Clarifying question)

This question is asked to help clarify what the person is saying. By getting them to clarify, you may actually give everyone a chance to see how silly it really sounds. For example, if your teacher says that dinosaurs evolved into birds, you could ask, "What do you mean by what you are saying? Do you mean that there was an animal that was half dinosaur and half bird? Could it fly? Could it fight with half-evolved wings? Were there lots of half and half's that died trying to fly before their wings were fully developed?'

2. How do you know what you are saying is true? (Asking for evidence)

This question will usually show that evolutionary beliefs are built on assumptions. If they say that rocks are billions of years old, you can ask, "How do you know that to be true?' Usually the answer to that question will be based on a belief instead of evidence, something like, "We believe that the earth is billions of years old." Again, you can ask how they know that to be true. After a while, it will become obvious that their answers are built on religious ideas, not facts.

3. If you are right, what does it mean? (Importance of their belief)

If your teacher makes the statement that mankind evolved from apes, you can simply ask, "If you are right, what does it mean?' This type of question will give the person a chance to tell why this belief is so important to them. It will help you to see their bias.

4. What if you are wrong about what you are saying? (Question of implications)

This question will allow the person to think through the consequences of being wrong. If they say that evolution is a proven fact, just ask, "What if you are wrong about what you are saying?" If they're honest, there are some major implications if evolution is not true and there really is a God who will hold them accountable for their actions! As a matter of fact, a great follow-up statement after asking this question may be something like, "It sounds like you're really risking some major consequences based on your assumptions!" Hopefully this will help the teacher or fellow students see how dangerous it is to place so much faith in something that is not trustworthy!

Remember, when you ask these questions be respectful with the motivation of love!

Evolution is a belief about the beginning of the universe that is based on ideas, and not facts. With a little practice, you can help others to see that evolution is merely a religious idea.

Likewise, you also have a faith, but it's not a blind-faith. It's a belief that is in harmony with the evidence, and given to us by the Eye-witness who was there from the beginning. As you learn the truth, it is important that you know the answers for what you believe. Could you answer the four questions about your faith? Remember to spend time in God's word. Then apply the four questions to your faith, and discuss them with your family. Remember what I Peter 3:15 says?

"But sanctify the Lord God in your hearts: and be ready always to give an answer to every man that asketh you a reason of the hope that is in you with meekness and fear."

Waves are familiar sights as you look around the environment you live in. You can see waves on a river, a lake, the ocean, or a flag waving in the wind. Both sound and light move through air as invisible waves.

What is sound? Sounds are vibrations---wavelike forms of energy.

What happens when you throw a stone into a still pond? It creates little waves that spread across the surface of the water. Sound also travels in waves. By making a disturbance, you can cause sound waves to ripple through the air.

Although sound travels in waves, it is actually a different type of wave than those that travel through water. Instead, it is a *longitudinal wave*, better known as a **P-wave**.

Activity—Exploring the P-wave

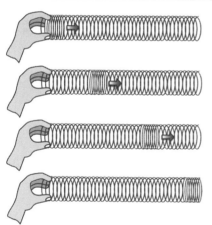

To understand how waves of sound travel through the air, place a slinky in a clear tube. Now on one end of the slinky, push it in and then back out very quickly, causing the slinky to bunch up at that end. This bunching is known as a compression. Now watch as that compression travels the entire length of the slinky.

Now let's try it again, creating several compressions. Move the end of the slinky back and forth several times. Watch how these "waves" of compression travel along the slinky. These are P-waves.

This is how sounds travel through the air. Something causes a compression of air molecules, which then sends waves of air compressions that travel away from the original source.

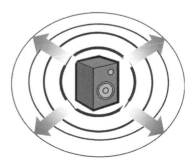

Making Sound

Since sounds are waves of compressions (or disturbances) traveling through the air, many things can make sound. When we hit a drum, it vibrates, creating sound waves. Objects can be vibrated by magnets, like in a radio speaker. Vibrating or moving air is also a common way to make sound. Wind causes the leaves of trees to vibrate. Moving air even makes our voices. We use air from our lungs to vibrate our vocal chords in order to make sound. Every person's vocal chords are shaped a little differently, so the vibrations that are made give each person a unique sounding voice.

Frequency

What is frequency?

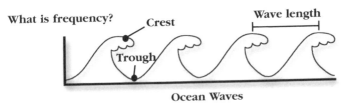

Ocean Waves

If you looked at the waves rolling onto the beach, the **frequency** would be how often a wave would hit the beach. Say that twelve waves rolled up onto the beach in a minute, the frequency would be 12 per minute. The distance between the waves is known as **wavelength**.

We can also measure the frequency of sound waves.

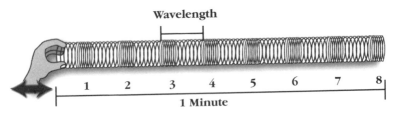

Remember our slinky example? The faster you moved the slinky back and forth, the closer together you could make the waves move along the slinky – which would increase the frequency. In the diagram, the frequency is 8 per minute.

Frequency is what controls the pitch of a sound. We are not talking about the sticky pitch found on a fir tree or pitching in a softball game! This type of pitch is the difference between a low note and a high note. Have you ever sung "do ray me fa so la ti do"? This starts at a low note and ends at a higher note. Notes that are low, such as the sound that a foghorn makes, have wavelengths that are far apart. Notes that are high, such as a referee whistle, have wavelengths that are very short

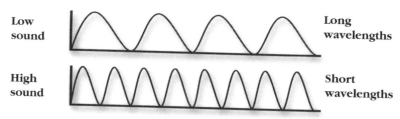

Low sound — Long wavelengths

High sound — Short wavelengths

This means that the frequency of a sound wave changes the pitch of the sound. Remember that pitch is talking about a high or low sound. The faster the frequency is, the higher the pitch (high note) is. The slower the frequency is, the lower the pitch (low note).

Comparing Waves

Light also travels as waves. Our eyes are designed to see certain wavelengths of light. This is called the visible spectrum. A rainbow is a spectrum of color. There are also many wavelengths of light that our eyes can not see. Just like there are many sounds that our ears can't hear.

The Design of the Human Ear

God made sound waves and the ear so that they would work together. Each part of the ear has a special job. When all the parts work together, the ear is healthy. If one of the parts is damaged or missing, a person can not hear normally or can't hear at all.

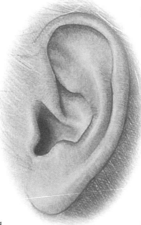

Evolutionists state that the ear evolved slowly, part by part, over time through the evolution of different animals. The evolution story says that it all began with the bones that support the gills of a fish. As this fish evolved into a reptile, the bones of its gills changed, becoming part of the reptile's jaw because the bones were no longer needed for the gills. The evolution story continues to say that as this reptile evolved into a mammal, some of the jawbones changed and became part of the ear of a mammal.

Creationists say that each kind of animal is especially made for where it lives and what it does. Each part of the animal has a job and was made fully formed and put together. What would the animal do that only had part of its jawbone? It couldn't eat. What would the animal do that only had part of its ear? It could not hear. So, it is important to see how each part of the ear has a job and how they all work together to make hearing happen.

The Human Ear and How Your Ear Hears Sound

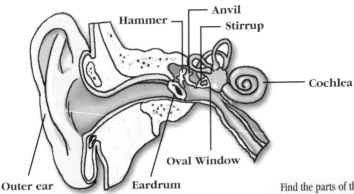

Anvil

Hammer

Stirrup

Cochlea

Oval Window

Outer ear

Eardrum

Find the parts of the ear as you read the description of how the ear hears.

A sound wave moves through the air, is captured by the ***outer ear***, is funneled to the ***eardrum***, and makes it vibrate. Next, the bones connected to the eardrum in the middle ear (***stirrup***, ***anvil***, and ***hammer***) vibrate. The pressure from these bones vibrating, push on the ***oval window***, which is a flexible elastic covering of the entrance to the inner ear, called the ***cochlea***. The cochlea has fluid and hair cells in it. The vibrations become waves in the fluid of the cochlea and the sensitive hair cells bend and move in response to the waves (like seaweed in the ocean). The hair cells are connected to nerves, which then talk with your brain about what is being heard.

Factoid
Humans have about 16,000 hair cells in the inner ear. Motion sickness happens when continuous motions overstimulate the hair cells.

Dare to Enter. . . "The Threshold of Hearing"

A decibel is the unit that is used to measure sound. Zero decibels are called "the threshold of hearing"---the faintest sounds that our ears can hear. The following is a list of sounds and the number of decibels that they measure.

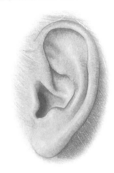

Decibels	Sound
0	Threshold of hearing
10-20	Whisper, Rustle of leaves
30-40	Buzz of a mosquito, Quiet radio
50	Moderate rainfall
60	Conversation, Dishwasher
70	Busy traffic, Vacuum cleaner
80	Alarm clock
90	Lawn mower
100	Chain saw
110	Rock music
	(an hour at this level will damage your hearing)
120-140	Jet plane take off
	(Damage and physical ear pain occur.)

Factoid
The most intense sound which the ear can safely hear is more than one billion times more intense than the faintest sounds humans can hear.

Tympani and Stapedius Muscles

These are muscles that God has made to protect our ear. When we are exposed to a sound that would damage our ear, the tensor tympani muscle pulls the hammer bone in, and the stapedius muscle pulls in the stirrup bone. By doing this, it dampens the loud sound like pressing your hand against a drum head, just as you hit it. Again, this shows God's loving design.

Bird Hearing

Bird hearing is specialized to be able to tell the difference in frequency between different birds' calls. Each bird type notices its own family's call more than any other type of bird's call. Birds are most sensitive to the sounds made by their own type of bird. This helps them to recognize each other and strangers.

One of the special features of a bird is that its cochlea is 1/10th the length of the cochlea in a mammal, but it has 10 times the number of hair cells. The more hair cells, the more sensitive the ear is to sound.

$$\begin{array}{r} 16{,}000 \text{ hair cells in a mammal} \\ \times \quad 10 \\ \hline 160{,}000 \text{ hair cells in a bird} \end{array}$$

Birds have about 160,000 hair cells in their inner ear which is smaller than humans', making them more sensitive to sound.

The Hearing Range of Mammals

Frequency is measured in a term called Hertz (Hz). Hertz is the number of times a sound vibrates in one second. 1 Kilohertz (kHz) is 1000 Hertz. The following table shows the highest frequency that certain mammals can hear.

Mammal	Highest Frequency Heard
Human	23kHz
Dog	45kHz
Cat	64kHz
Bat	110kHz
Porpoise	150kHz

In the Spotlight— The OWL

Offset ears

Prey

Owls are the more sensitive to sounds than other birds. Their ears are as sensitive as a cat's. Some owls can catch prey in total darkness by only using their hearing. A special feature that owls have is asymmetrical or offset external ear openings that help to locate their food. Since owls are usually resting in trees, this feature of their ears helps them to be able to know not only the distance away that they hear the food, but also the distance below on the forest floor.

God's Ears

What do you think that God's ears are like? What do you think that God hears? Psalm 69:34 says, "Let heaven and earth praise Him. The seas and everything that moves in them." Psalm 89:5 says, "And the heavens will praise your wonders, O Lord." Psalm 145:21 says, "My mouth shall speak the praise of the Lord, and all flesh shall bless His holy name forever and ever." Do you think that God hears all the sounds that are made? Do you think that He sees every color that He made? Wow, can you imagine the amazing harmonies that God must hear from all of His creation?

God's Love

Have you ever thought of how God made our ears just right for us? He made our ears to do so many things that we need to help us to survive. They protect us when we hear something dangerous coming our way. We use them to communicate with others, and to enjoy the beautiful sounds of His creation.

He also made them perfectly matched for us. Just think if the human hearing range had evolved? What if our voices had evolved in a range that was outside our human hearing range (like a bat's voice)? Or what if we had a larger hearing range, and we could hear constant high-pitched noises, or low noises that would always be annoying. No, instead God created us to hear in the perfect range. What a loving Creator!

Bible Lesson

Our ears are specially made by God to provide for us and to protect us. Many times Jesus says in the Bible "for him who has ears to hear". We all have ears, but some people are open to hearing spiritual truths more than others are. Hearing God's voice is just as important or more important as physically hearing each other. Romans 10:7 says, "So then faith cometh by hearing, and hearing by the word of God." Hearing the word of God provides for us and protects us!

I Timothy 6:10 says, "For the love of money is the root of all evil: which while some coveted after, they have erred from the faith, and pierced themselves through with many sorrows." If we have ears to hear, this verse gives us a warning to protect us. Money and evil sometimes go hand in hand. We have to be careful not to love money or the pursuit of it more than we love God.

Take time to listen to and read God's word and you will hear God's still small voice speaking to you.

'In the beginning God created the heavens and the earth"

This is a familiar phrase. Have you thought about what it really means? Yes, He really did create everything! He put thought into making each plant, animal and human. Let's look closely at the verses in Genesis that explain God creating animals and humans.

Genesis 1:20-21 *"And God said, Let the waters bring forth <u>abundantly the moving creature that hath life</u>, and <u>fowl</u> that may fly above the earth in the open firmament of heaven. And God created <u>great whales</u>, and <u>every living creature that moveth, which the waters brought forth abundantly</u>, after their kind, and every winged fowl after his kind: and God saw that it was good."*

Genesis 1:24-25 *"And God said, Let the earth bring forth the living creature after his kind, <u>cattle</u>, and <u>creeping thing</u>, and <u>beast of the earth</u> after his kind: and it was so. And God made the beast of the earth after his kind, and cattle after their kind, and every thing that creepeth upon the earth after his kind: and God saw that it was good."*

Genesis 1:26-27 *"And God said, Let us make <u>man</u> in our image, after our likeness: and let them have dominion over the fish of the sea, and over the fowl of the air, and over the cattle, and over all the earth, and over every creeping thing that creepeth upon the earth. So God created man in his own image, in the image of God created he him; <u>male and female</u> created he them."*

According to these scriptures there are 6 categories of living things that God created:
1. Sea Creatures- large and small
2. Birds
3. Cattle- This word refers to not just cows but livestock (animals on a farm).
4. Creeping Things-All animals that crawl or creep on the ground.
5. Beasts-large and small wild animals
6. Mankind

Make a list of every animal that you can think of and place each animal within one of the categories described in Genesis.
Your List May Include:

1. **Sea creatures**	2. **Birds**	3. **Cattle**	4. **Creeping**	5. **Beasts**
Dolphin	Blue Heron	Sheep	Rat	Lion
Whales	Humming bird	Cow	Insects	Monkey
Fish	Crow	Pig	Snake	Bear
Octopus	Duck	Goats	Alligator	Elk
Sea slug	Owl			Moose
Clam	Eagle			

6. **Mankind**
   Male and female

What about Dinosaurs, what category do they fit in?

53

Every animal that you listed can fit into one of the categories described by Genesis. There is no new kind of animal. God designed each type of animal at the beginning of creation. God even planned out how He would make mankind.

Humans are God's unique creation. We are the only creation that God made in his own image, in His likeness. Notice that God did not say that about the sea creatures or the wild beasts even though sometimes we would like them to be like us! This is important to understand. It shows us that we are very valuable and that we can have a relationship with God because he gave us the ability to know Him.

Who am I?

Creation A: My type eats a variety of food from insects to fruit and frogs.

Creation B: I grow to about an average of 6 feet in length.

Creation C: I can not see in the dark.

Classification of Animals

Classification means to organize things into groups. This makes it is easier to study and talk about them.

Fun Activity

Let's look at clothes buttons. Does your mother or grandmother have a button collection? If so, ask if she'll let you borrow them for this activity. If you don't have real buttons that you can use, draw or photocopy the picture of the buttons (below), cut them out and arrange them in to groups that have the same qualities.

There are different ways to group these buttons. How can you group them? What characteristics could you use?

You could group them by color, loop or no loop, number of holes, and the shape. Try to classify these buttons. Put them into groups that have like qualities.

This is similar to classifying animals.
Now let's look at some animals. How would you group these animals? Make a list.
Find their similarities (things that are the same) and differences.

Tiger	Hippo	Mosquito	Turtle	Lion
Ostrich	Beetle	Toucan	Giraffe	Alligator
Elephant	Spider	Cheetah	Snake	

Here are some familiar ways that scientists group animals.

Reptile qualities	**Mammal qualities**	**Insect qualities**	**Bird qualities**
Scales	Skin with hair	Exoskeleton	Feathers
Give birth as eggs	Give live birth	Six legs	Beak
Cold blooded	Feed young milk	Three body section	Give birth as eggs

Can you answer these questions about the animals listed at the top of this page?

Which animals are large cats? → lion, tiger, cheetah

Which animals are birds? → toucan, ostrich

Which animals are reptiles? → alligator, turtle, snake

Which animals are insects? → mosquito, beetle (a spider is not an insect)

Which animals are mammals? → Giraffe, elephant, hippo, tiger, cheetah, lion

Who am I?

Creation A: I literally fly with my hands.

Creation B: I communicate with sonar.

Creation C: I am a mammal.

How a Scientist Classifies Animals

1. Scientists begin to classify living things by first placing them in a large category called a Kingdom. There is one Kingdom represented in our list above. They are all in the Kingdom Animalia. This means that they are all animals.

2. The next category is called a phylum (pronounced fy-lum) This is a smaller group and members of certain Phyla have certain qualities.

3. This grouping continues until a specific animal is given a 'species' name.

Classification Categories

Kingdom

Phylum

Class

Order

Family

Genius

Species

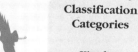

Let's look at the example of the western diamondback rattlesnake (Crotalus atrox). The names seem strange because they are written in Latin:

Kingdom- Animalia
Phylum- Chordata
Class- Reptilia
Order- Squamata
Family- Viperidea
Genus- Crotalus
Species- Atrox

This process of classification can become very complicated because there are so many living things all over the world.

Different biomes include areas like:

Deserts (D)
Savanna (S)
Grasslands (G)
Scrub brushlands (Sc)
Mountains (M)

Tundra (T)
Tropical rain forests (TR)
Boreal forests (BF)
Temperate forest (TF)
Temperate rain forest (TRF)

Four different types of forests

Study the map.

Where are the different biomes located?

What type of biomes are found where you live?

What type of biomes are found in Africa?

Animals and their Habitats

Animals are specifically suited for the environment that they live in. Some people call this 'specialized'. Almost every nook and cranny of the world has some living creature that has filled it. God gave man and animals the ability to "reproduce after its own kind" Genesis 1:25 and commanded them to multiply and 'fill the earth'.

What does it mean for an animal to be specialized?
It means that it lives in a certain place, eats certain things, and is used to a certain climate.

God has designed the animal to fit and adapt into its environment. Adapt means to adjust as needed. God designed each animal to be able to adjust to its environment. It is dependant on the place it lives to provide its needs.

The earth has many biomes or areas for animals to live in. A biome is a large area of land that has certain plants, animals, and climate conditions.

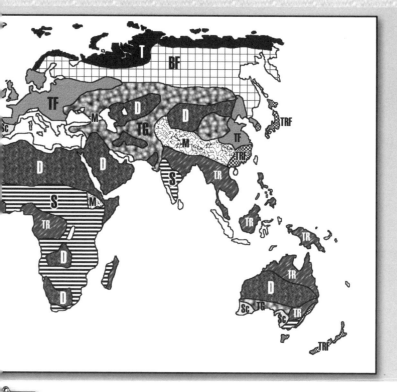

What's the point?

It is important to understand how the animal and its habitat fit together. There is a purpose and a direction. Evolutionists would say that the type of animal randomly, by chance evolved the qualities necessary for it to survive in the environment. Creationists would say that the animal's ability to adapt to its environment is designed and purposed by God.

A tool to use to help you defend your faith is called a design argument. This means that you can point out things in nature that are designed by God. They are amazing puzzle pieces that fit perfectly together. Animals are specialized to live in their habitat. Without these special attributes they would not be able to live.

Keep your eyes peeled for these design features!

King of the Jungle—Lion

Location: Africa
Ability: leap 40feet in one pounce

A true story:

There are many tribes of bush people in Tanzania, East Africa. They are called bush people because they live in very remote far away places and some tribes make houses and fences out of the dry bushes in the area that they live. Many have a language that sounds like clicking with the tongue against the roof of your mouth. Two missionaries were visiting a tribe of bush people in Tanzania. They were camping in a tent inside a bush family's fenced compound. The fence was about 12 feet high and encircled the house. At night, they bring their livestock inside the fence (goats and cows) to protect them from being eaten. One night they slept soundly in the tent. In the morning they were told a story about something that happened as they were sleeping. Someone saw a very large lion silently jump over the 12 foot high fence and grab a cow in its jaws and jump back over the fence and run away. The lion did not bother any people; he just wanted a good cow for a meal. This is a great example of the silent strength of the King of the Jungle.

How did that lion know where to go to find a cow for his dinner?

Lions and several other types of animals, have what is called the Jacobson's organ. It is named after the person who discovered it. This design feature helps the lion find its food. Jacobson's organs are chemically sensitive nerve endings that are found in two 'pits' on the inside of the roof of the mouth. The lion lifts his upper lip and breathes in the air. This gives the lion an extra sensitive sense of smell. You may have seen your pet cat lift its upper lip and breathe. It is using the same sense of extra smell.

How could that lion see in the middle of the night?

The Creator designed lions so they can see in the dark. Aside from large eyes, God also gave them a very special design. Many other mammals and some fish have a design feature that is called the tapetum lucidum. Have you ever seen the reflection in a cat, deer, or dog's eyes when a flashlight or car headlight shines on them? To help some animals see in the dark God invented a special feature that is like a mirror in the eye. The tapetum lucidum, is a layered membrane inside the back of the eye. When the dim light of darkness (even in darkness there is a little light) enters the eye it is reflected again back into the retina (light absorbing part of the eye) making it brighter, thus making the animal able to see in the dark.

More than a fashion statement!

Why does the lion have whiskers? Using their whiskers, lions can actually feel vibrations on the ground or in the air. This helps them to get around at night. Using them as "feelers", whiskers help the lion locate the "perfect bite" on their prey. These whiskers also trap scent particles that help its Jacobson's organ do its job of super-smell. Finally, whiskers display the lion's mood.

Other Special Features

Lions have more muscle and lighter bones than other animals its size. This allows them to run up to 40 miles per hour, jump 12 feet high, and leap 40 feet in one pounce! God made its claws so they can retract up into its paws when it's not using them. With the pads on the bottom of its feet, it gives it the ability to be very quiet when it sneaks up on prey. Even though the lion can be very quiet, it can also make a very loud noise – its roar can be heard up to 5 miles away! The lion also has a specially designed tongue. It has spines that allow the lion to scrape the meat off of bones. God has truly made the lion to be a mighty hunter!

Write two design features in which the lion was made.

- _____
- _____

What a long neck you have Giraffe!

Location: Africa
Size: Neck up to 10 feet long

Special features:

The giraffe has several special features that make it unique. Each of these features is a piece of the puzzle that makes it a whole giraffe. Kind of like the pattern on its fur! Without one of these pieces the animal would not be able to live like it does. Because of the giraffes amazing size, it has a unique system to pump its blood and to breathe.

Circulatory system (used to pump its blood)

- extra large heart needed to pump its blood up its long neck
- giraffe's heart pumps blood 2 times as strong as most animals
- by the time the blood travels up the long neck, the blood pressure that arrives at the giraffe's brain is normal
- since the blood pressure is high through the rest of its body, God has given the giraffe special skin to tolerate the pressure, especially in the bottom of its legs
- special valves in its neck to keep its blood pressure from bursting vessels or damaging its brain when the giraffe bends over to get a drink of water

Respiratory system (used for breathing)

- extra large lungs
- breathes slowly so the air has time to travel up its long neck

Which has more bones in its neck a tiger, a bat, or a giraffe?   (They each have the same number, 7.)

Don't hide your head in the sand Ostrich!
Location: Africa, South America (Rhea), Australia (Emu)
Size: Up to nine feet tall and can weigh up to 350 pounds

Do ostriches really hide their heads in the sand? No, they do not.
Do you know the expression of having eyes bigger than your stomach?
Well the ostrich literally has eyes that are bigger than its brain! And
has two set of eyelids that protect its eyes. One set is similar to ours
and the other set blinks from the sides to keep out sand during
sand storms. Ostriches mostly eat plants but also some insects,
fruits, seeds, nuts, and small lizards. Ostriches can not fly, but
are specialized to run fast! It has very powerful legs, knees that
bend in the opposite direction as do humans knees, and two-toes on its
feet. All these qualities enable it to run about 45 miles per hour—that is the fastest two-
legged animal! It's thought that ostriches can maintain top-speed for up to 30 minutes!

Yes you can, Toucan!
Color me!
Location: Tropical areas
**Size: Best known for its large yellow,
orange, red, green and black beak.**

Its beak is so large it appears that it would be too heavy for
the bird to fly or it would just tip over. This beak is made of
thin, lightweight material and has air pockets in side it. It uses its
beak for eating and attracting a mate. The toucan can turn his head
around, rest its beak on his back, and fold his tail up over its head when it sleeps!

The Keel-billed toucan is the national bird of Belize, South America. Its beak is specialized to
feed on a variety of tropical forest fruits, some insects, reptiles and bird eggs. They nest in
holes in trees, lay one to four eggs, and make a sound that resembles a frog.

The Hippo and Its Snorkeling Equipment

Location: Africa
**Ability: swim with their eyes,
ears, and nostrils above water.**

Special features:
- snorkel equipment   -3 stomachs   -natural water proof sunscreen.

The hippo's snorkeling equipment includes eyes, nostrils, and ears that are on the top of its head
so that they can swim in the water with just the very top of their head out of the water. When they
do go under water their nostrils close, and their ears fold back to keep the water out.

Hippopotamuses are part of the ungulate group of animals like cows. They chew their cud and
have more than one stomach. The stomachs are necessary to digest the plant material that they
eat and get all the possible nutrients. Hippos would not get enough nutrients if they did not have
three stomachs.

God has made hippos with natural sun-block. From their skin oozes a thick, oily liquid that
keeps it from getting sunburned. Not only that, but this sunscreen is waterproof!

Mystery at McBane Manor - part 2

My, what a big nose you have Elephant!
Location: Africa, India
Size: Average weight is 6.6 tons

Every animal has a way to keep themselves cool.

Dogs pant.

People sweat.

Elephants flap their ears.

The elephants sophisticated trunk:
- is made with 40,000 muscles
- its like a water bottle for holding water for when it is thirsty – it can hold up to 4 gallons of water
- can suck up mud or dust and spray it onto the elephant to stay cool
- has two finger-like parts at the end to pick up things and use to eat
- is strong enough to lift a tree trunk, yet handy enough to pick a blade of grass
- used for communicating

Did you think that elephants flapped their ears to fly in the air? Well, elephants flap their ears to keep themselves cool. The air cools the blood vessels with in the ear; this lowers the elephant's body temperature. It works a bit like a radiator in a car.

Another way that the Creator designed the elephant to stay cool is its skin. Have you ever noticed how wrinkly it is? When it sprays itself with water, it gets trapped in those wrinkles so it doesn't just roll of its back. When the water evaporates, it cools the elephant down.

Elephants also have incredible hearing. They can hear sounds that are much lower than we can. They can also communicate over very long distances.

Have you ever looked at the big, flat feet of the elephant? God has designed them with special elastic, spongy cushions in their soles. This allows them to support all their weight, and move quietly.

Tusks are an important tool for the elephant. They use them to pry the bark off of trees, digging down for roots, and they also use them as a defense. While humans get two sets of teeth over their lifetime, God has designed elephants to get six because of all the rough things they eat !

MYSTERY CREATION

? ? ?
A B C

Who am I?

Creation A: I can eat 600 mosquitoes in an hour.
Creation B: I can hold my breath 5-8 minutes at a time.
Creation C: I have 200 bones in my body.

My, what big teeth you have, Snake!

Habitat: Sea level to 7000ft. ranging from deserts to rocky hillsides, grassy meadows and forested areas.

The snake's scales:
- aren't individual pieces like on a fish
- are made from hundreds of folds in their skin
- protect the snake like a set of armor
- this design allows the scales to stretch as the snake slithers and moves
- this design also gives the snake traction like tread on a tire

The snake's eyes:
- are covered by clear scales to protect its eyesight

The snake's jaw:
- is made so that the lower jaw isn't connected to the rest so it can open wide to swallow large meals

The snake's ribs:
- are made so that they can expand as they swallow their prey

The snake's tongue:
- picks up dust particles and brings it inside its mouth, past the Jacobson's organ to give the snake a super sense of smell (Gen 3:14, *"And the LORD God said unto the serpent, Because thou hast done this, thou art cursed above all cattle, and above every beast of the field; upon thy belly shalt thou go, and dust shalt thou eat all the days of thy life:"*)

Mozambique Cobra
One of the most amazing snakes is the Mozambique Cobra. Its venom is strong enough to cause instant blindness, and even death in some cases. It has the ability to spit this venom up to eight feet!

Rattle Snake
Rattle snakes can be very dangerous snakes. The western diamondback can grow to over 7 feet long. It has heat-sensing pits in front of its eyes that act basically as infrared sensors allowing the snake to 'see' in the dark and find any warm blooded prey. These pits help to regulate the amount of venom that is released in order to kill its prey.

Do snakes ever blink their eyes? No. The rattlesnake has lidless eyes that are protected by a clear outer skin layer. Its rattle is used to warn and scare off things that come near.

Test Your Rattlesnake Knowledge.

Answer true or false

1. Rattlesnakes have legs.
2. Rattlesnakes blink their eyes.
3. Rattlesnakes can 'see' in the dark.
4. Rattlesnakes are poisonous.

Answer: 1. false 2. false 3. true 4. true

My, what hairy legs you have Spider!

There have been estimates that there are over 36,000 different species of spiders! Only about 30 of those are dangerous to humans. God has made our world in such a wonderful balance, and spiders play a large part of that. Without spiders, cockroaches, flies, and other pests would overtake our planet!

Spider webs:
- are made by liquid silk that is pumped into a special gland of the spider's body called a spinneret, that weaves the silk into these familiar shapes.
- are made in several different ways by different species of spiders. They make:

Triangle webs   **Orb webs**   **Sheet webs**   **Tangle webs**

Spiders are not insects. Do you know why?

One difference is that insects have six legs and spiders have eight legs. Tarantulas are very interesting spiders and some people keep them as pets. Sizes range from a fingernail to a dinner plate. They live in rainforests and deserts. They eat insects, rodents, and sometimes baby birds and reptiles.

They catch their food by slowly creeping up to it and then quickly pouncing on to the food and stick their hollow fangs into it and inject venom that turns the insides of the prey into liquid! EEEWWW Don't worry!! The venom from most spiders can not kill people unless you are allergic to it.

Spiders

8 legs, 2 body segments

Insects

6 legs, 3 body segments

Amazing Spiders

Spitting Spiders
Some spiders have a creative way of catching prey that is too fast for it to catch. They can spit its sticky venom to glue its victim in place!

Traps
Some spiders actually make traps so that their prey sets off a trip-line, yanking the insect up into the air, left dangling at the spider's mercy!

Tarantulas
There are tarantulas that throw the hairs of its abdomen or the back of its legs at its enemy. The hairs stick to the enemy and cause them to itch or give them pain. Each hair is covered with tiny sharp points.

Spider Hair
So why do most other spiders also have hair? In many cases those hairs are surrounded by very sensitive nerves. This allows spiders to detect vibrations that are happening all around them to protect them from danger, or help them detect their prey.

MYSTERY CREATION Clues

A   B   C

Throughout this section of the study guide, we've placed 3 Mystery Creations. These are clues to help you discover the identity of each of those animals if you haven't already figured them out.

Now, list similarities and differences between the different arms in the diagram. After you know what type of living things that the mystery creations are, answer the following question:

What are the purposes of each type of arm design?

(The purposes are very different and specific. One is for flying, one is for swimming and the other is for hugging!) A similar design and specific purpose points us to a creator who designed it.

Compare the three arms

Creation A:

Creation B:

Creation C:

MYSTERY CREATION Answers

A bat   A dolphin   A human

Let's tell the world about the Creator!

Every animal is so unique. Make sure that you appreciate all created things. However, as a human made in God's image, we are so valuable to Him. You are the most valuable aspect of creation. Christ made the ultimate sacrifice for you. He paid your penalty, which is death, for sin. Animals where not given that opportunity. He did not need to be crucified for the choice animals made but only for man's choice. This awesome and amazing Creator chose to love you. It is important for us to "go ye therefore, and teach all nations" (Matthew 28:19) of this good news. Have you thought about being a missionary when you grow up? It can be around the world, or right now in your neighborhood!

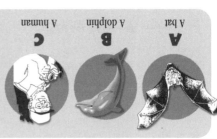

The Great Flood

As you probably know, the Bible talks about a huge flood that covered the entire earth. It killed all animals, plants, and people that were not on the ark that God instructed Noah to build. Why would God bring such destruction to the earth? Genesis 6:5-8 says, *"And God saw that the wickedness of man was great in the earth, and that every imagination of the thoughts of his heart was only evil continually. And it repented the LORD that he had made man on the earth, and it grieved him at his heart. And the LORD said, I will destroy man whom I have created from the face of the earth; both man, and beast, and the creeping thing, and the fowls of the air; for it repenteth me that I have made them. But Noah found grace in the eyes of the LORD."* Why would God want Noah to build such a huge boat? It was so that animal and human life would be saved from the Flood.

Do you know how long the time of the flood lasted? Although it rained for forty days and nights, Genesis 7:24 says that water prevailed on the earth for 150 days. It was months after that until the water finally receded from the face of the earth. As a matter of fact, the total time for the flood to come and then go away was just over one year!

What Happened to the Earth during the Flood?

Genesis tells us a few things that happened to the earth. In Genesis 7:11 we read, *"In the six hundredth year of Noah's life, in the second month, the seventeenth day of the month, the same day were all the fountains of the great deep broken up, and the windows of heaven were opened."* This means two things. First, fountains of water that were underground came up. Second, earthquakes and possibly volcanoes may have exploded in order to break up the earth's crust. Scripture says that this went on for five months. So much of the earth was broken up and became a muddy mess. As the waters began to drain away, things that were broken up began to settle down.

So What Happened to the Plants and Animals that Died During the Flood?

Imagine what was happening during the flood. There were probably hurricanes, tidal waves, and raging currents of water. These powerful water forces must've picked up huge amounts of rock material, and animals and deposited them in huge piles all around the earth! Many of these animals became preserved in the layers of soil in which they were buried. The flood provided the conditions necessary for plants and animals to become petrified or fossilized. (A petrified organism is one whose cells have been replaced with minerals. A fossil is any evidence of life that has been preserved in rock.)

Petrification

It's common to find petrified wood. Petrification of wood is a process that needs very specific conditions:

First, a tree must be protected from decay. This means that it must be buried quickly by mud.

Second, water in the mud must have minerals in it such as silica which is released when water mixes with volcanic ash.

Third, because the wood is spongy, it soaks up the mineral-filled water.

Wood soaking up water is like a kitchen sponge soaking up water. A sponge is porous; it has holes all over it. When the sponge is dry, the holes soak up the water and the water fills it.

Wood
Cell

Notice how the porous wood is just like a sponge.

If these requirements are met, the growth of mineral crystals begins in the porous cell walls of the wood. Eventually the silica replaces the wood cells, and the tree becomes preserved as a rock.

Wood can become different colors depending on the mineral that is replacing the cells of the wood. Colors of petrified wood can range from green, to brown, red, white, pink, and blue.

Plants and Animals Can Also Be Called Fossils.

Fossils are remains or traces of plants and animals preserved in rock. The process of becoming a fossil starts when plants or animals are buried under a lot of heavy mud. Gradually, the soft parts of the plants or animals rot away and the hard parts like teeth, bones, and shells become like rock.

Types of Fossils

The following list shows a number of names for different types of fossils.

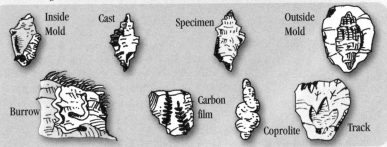

1. Specimen (an actual object of study)
2. Mold (an outline in rock)
3. Carbon film (a thin black carbon sheet that is left from a flat living thing like a leaf or a fish)
4. Coprolite (fossilized animal droppings)
5. Track (an imprint of an animal footprint)
6. Burrow (a preserved nest or a trail of an animal such as a worm would make)

What conditions are best for the making of a fossil?

Will a lizard buried by mud or a fish left exposed on a riverbank be more likely to become a fossil? Why?

Activity: Making Your Own Fossil Replicas

Sometimes when you go to a museum and see dinosaur bones or other fossils, they are not the actual fossil. Since they want to protect the valuable fossils, they place copies of those fossils on display called fossil replicas. Now you have your own chance to make fossil replicas:

To do this activity you will need:
Plaster of Paris
A shallow or disposable pie tin
Clay
Objects that you want to fossilize

Follow this procedure:
Press a 1/4 inch layer of clay into the bottom of the pie tin. (Mud that is the consistency of clay can also work in place of clay.) Gently but firmly press several objects into the clay so that they leave an imprint in the clay. Shells, ferns, bones, and other such objects work well.

Next, remove the objects from the clay, and then leave the clay to dry overnight.

When the clay is dry, mix about two cups of Plaster of Paris following the directions given on the package. Pour the mixture into the pie tin over the impressions in the clay, and let the plaster harden.

When it is no longer damp to the touch, carefully peel away the pie tin and clay from the Plaster of Paris and examine the fossil imprints you made!

Did Noah's Flood Really Happen?

Let's look for evidence! Put on that investigative hat and we're off!

Evidence Location #1: A place called Ghost Ranch shows evidence of a flood.

Ghost Ranch is a ranch of 21,000 acres in New Mexico. It was originally called Piedra Lumbre (Shining Rock), but over time because of legends from cattle rustlers and others in the area, the name became Ghost Ranch. Arthur and Phoebe Pack gave the ranch to the Presbyterian Church in 1955. Today it is a conference center with a museum and a farm. It became a place of interest for scientists when thousands of Coelophysis dinosaur fossils (see picture) were discovered there. To show that the flood talked about in the Bible is true, it is helpful to find real evidence of the Flood today. Ghost Ranch offers some wonderful evidence.

Evidence A: The Chinle formation is a rock layer that stretches through six western states. It is a large layer of volcanic ash and mudstone.

A layer of rock covering such a large area shows scientists that there was a huge catastrophe that stretched over a massive area.

Evidence B: At Ghost Ranch there are thousands of Coelophysis dinosaur fossils covered by the Chinle formation. Scientists working at the site believe those dinosaurs were killed by water. It is interesting to notice that

- many Coelophysis are buried in a jumbled mess
- these fossils look like they were deposited somewhere else, and then ripped-up and re-deposited
  at Ghost Ranch
- some are buried in neck-wrenching positions
- some are buried facing in the same direction like
  a current of water would have arranged them.

This evidence shows that lots of powerful water was involved in the burial of these dinosaurs.

Evidence C: Coelophysis fossils at Ghost Ranch show no signs of exposure or erosion.

This means that if the animals died and were left out in the open before being gradually buried, they'd be a little worn. So instead, these fossils must have been buried quickly.

Evidence D: Lungfish have been found buried with the Coelophysis fossils.

Finding water-dwelling animals like lungfish mixed in with land-dwelling animals suggests that there must have been a large amount of water that picked up animals from different places, and mixed them all together.

Ghost Ranch evidences support that the Biblical flood really happened.

Evidence Location #2: Petrified Forest National Park, Arizona

The Petrified Forest is located in Northern Arizona. There are thousands of beautifully colored petrified logs. Do you remember what petrified means? The logs have completely turned into rock. Some of the trees are over 200 feet long and 10 feet in diameter. The trees are not standing upright but are lying on the ground. This forest is very different from a normal forest. Most of the logs do not have branches, bark, or roots. Another amazing thing you'll find here are bees' nests and burrows.

Evidence E: The logs are found in the Chinle rock layer just like at Ghost Ranch. There are tons and tons of logs on top of the ground and that much and more buried in the ground!

So the ingredients to make the logs petrified were all there: water, volcanic ash, and mud. These are the ingredients that would be there during Noah's flood.

Evidence F: The logs do not have their branches, bark, or roots.

If the trees were growing where they were buried, and were slowly covered with soil, the branches, roots, and bark should still be attached to the logs. It makes sense that if there was a flood, as the water rushed by the trees, they would be uprooted and the branches and bark ripped off by the strong water currents.

Evidence G: No Humus!

Do you know what humus is? Humus is actually a layer of soil on the forest floor. Humus is made of tree parts, like leaves, needles, and bark which have fallen onto the ground under a tree. The Petrified Forest is missing the layer of humus that should have been on the forest floor.

soil profile

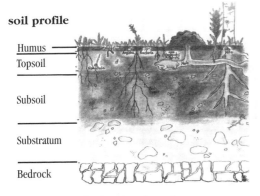

The drawing shows the layers that you would find if you went into a forest and began digging a hole straight down. This is called a *soil profile*. It shows you what layers animals live in, how far down the roots of a tree will grow, and the types of soil until you reach solid rock called *bedrock*.

What does it mean that there is no humus?

Since humus is found where trees grow in a forest and there is no humus, this suggests that the trees did not grow where the petrified logs are found today.

Mount St. Helen's

On May 18, 1980 a catastrophic event happened at Mount St. Helen's in Washington State. A huge landslide and explosion of steam blasted out over Spirit Lake at the base of the mountain. It made a water wave 860 feet high and blew down one million trees and deposited them into the lake. The blast ripped the trees out of the ground, leaving their roots and blowing off their branches.

Activity: Picture Hunt

See if you can find the following things in the picture.

1. Six logs floating up and down.
2. Layers of ash, branches, and bark
3. An elk

The logs, which are now floating in the lake, float vertically (up and down) in the water. One end, the root end, is heavier than the top. As they float for a while, they begin to get water-logged and their bark is rubbed off, and the logs then sink, still straight up and down, to the bottom in a standing position as if planted there.

Amazingly, different types of trees float longer than others. The noble firs were the first trees to sink down to the bottom of the lake, then the silver firs, then hemlock, and then others. In the meantime bark, branches, and ash were settling at the bottom with the logs creating different layers.

Can you observe the things above in the picture?

In Yellowstone there are petrified forests. The trees there at Specimen Ridge have been interpreted through evolutionary glasses. Some evolutionists claim that there are 27 layers of forests buried in sediment. That interpretation says that each layer of petrified logs was once a forest. Over long periods of time the forest eventually died out and more sediment covered it over. Then they believe that a new forest grew on top of the old one. There are many layers - 50 in some places, therefore, there were supposedly many different forests over thousands of years. So evolutionists say that the trees grew where they are found today.

Now, remember some of the qualities you learned about the petrified logs:

-Their roots were broken off at the ground level.
-Many of the trees are without bark or branches.
-The humus layer is missing in most areas.

Activity: Reinterpreting an Evolutionary Story

According to what you have learned about Petrified Forest National Park and Mount St. Helen's, reinterpret the petrified forest at Yellowstone through the eyes of a creation scientist by answering the following questions:

1. Are the petrified forests at Yellowstone like the one at the Petrified Forest National Park? How are they the same?

2. Are the layers of Yellowstone's petrified forest similar to those layers of trees being made at Mount St. Helen's?

3. Do the logs at the Petrified Forest, Yellowstone, and Mount St. Helen's have similar qualities? List two:

Creation, Evolution, & Time

Compare the creation and evolution timelines below for information about life and the earth's early history.

Creation Diagram		Evolution Diagram	
Time	**Happenings**	**Time**	**Happenings**
About 600 years ago		4.5 billion years ago	Earth came into being
Day 1	Heavens, Earth, Light	500 million years ago	Small sea creatures
Day 2	Firmament	400 million years ago	Fish
Day 3	Land, **Plants, Trees**	360-280 million years ago	Amphibians
Day 4	Sun, Moon, Stars	**200 - 220 million years ago**	**Insects, BEES, firs and pines**
Day 5	Sea creatures and Birds	**220 million years ago**	**Petrified Forest**
Day 6	**Creeping things,** and Beasts/Mankind	220-100 million years ago	Dinosaurs-reptiles
Day 7	Rest	**100 million years ago**	**Flowering plants**
After creation	Sin/Death enters the world	About 65-1.65 million years ago	Mammals/Mankind
About 4,000 years ago	The Flood, layers of the earth made	Today	Earthquakes and volcanoes happen once in a while.
Today	Earthquakes and volcanoes once in a while		

You can see that the amount of time in each table is very different. According to our chart, it took God 7 days to create all things, and it took evolution 4.5 billion years to evolve everything. This is a huge conflict between evolution and the Bible's account of creation.

Fossilized Beehives: So What about the Bees?

Fossilized beehives have been found in the petrified trees at the Petrified Forest. This is very exciting!! This is important evidence in favor of creation.

Evolutionists believe that the Petrified Forest is about 220 million years old. That would mean that the fossilized beehives are also that old since they are found within the petrified trees. The problem is that bees eat nectar from flowering plants.

But looking at the timeline, flowering plants did not supposedly evolve until **after** the time of the bees and the petrified trees. So, what did the bees eat if flowering plants did not evolve until more than 100 million years after the bees?

What's the point?

How did the bees survive without the food that they were designed to eat? The biblical account of creation makes much more sense than saying that bees lived for millions of years without flowers!

The Life and Times of Bees

Honeybees are social insects living in colonies. There are three distinctions of the bees that live in any colony. The Queen bee, the drones, and the worker bees. The Queen bee is the only fully developed female in the colony and is the one who lays eggs. She can lay about 1,200-3,000 eggs a day!

The drone bee's only purpose is to mate with the Queen. If the colony is short on food, the drones are the first to be kicked out of the nest!

Worker bees are the underdeveloped females. There can be 50,000-60,000 worker bees in a colony. The workers feed the Queen and the larvae, guard the entrance to the nest, and collect nectar to make honey.

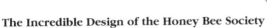

The Incredible Design of the Honey Bee Society

Suppose you are a beekeeper working with a colony of bees. You can observe some incredible things that God designed for the honeybee.

- The workers bring back nectar in specialized honey-stomachs.
- They use highly complex dances to communicate to other bees the location of nectar and flowers.
- Some worker bees use specialized mouth parts to make the wax for the nest.
- The hexagonal (six-sided) shape of a honeycomb cell is the most efficient shape for holding honey. It uses less wax than other shapes.

What about the Fossilized Bee Nests?

Remarkably the fossilized nests are very similar to nests made by ground nesting honeybees today. Each nest has clusters of 15-30 cells. Nests are made up of layers of flask-shaped cells arranged in circular patterns. Bees put one egg in each cell, with pollen and resin to nourish the larvae that hatches from the egg.

Fossil nests have features that exist in bee nests today, including spiral caps on the nests and a fancy arrangement of plant pieces lining the inside of the nest cells.

Fossilized bees seem to be the same as bees are today. This makes sense because God created them and designed them during the creation week.

Summary

Noah's Flood lasted about one year. Most of what the earth looks like today happened during Noah's Flood and shortly after. The layers of sediment of the earth were laid down by the flood-waters and buried animals and plants. Ghost Ranch, Petrified National Forest, Yellowstone National Park, and Mount St. Helen's all show evidence for the worldwide Flood of Noah.

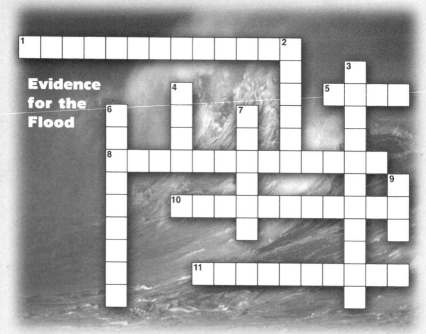

Evidence for the Flood

DOWN

2 A mineral found in volcanic ash.

3 A place where there are many layers of trees on top of each other.

4 The amount of time that Noah's Flood lasted.

6 Fossilized animal droppings.

7 A rock layer that stretches over 6 states.

9 Comes out of a volcano.

ACROSS

1 A recent volcano.

5 Animals that live in colonies.

8 A process that changes wood cells into rock.

10 A type of dinosaur fossil.

11 A place where evidence for the Flood is found.

Puzzle Answer

I Corinthians 15:58: *"Therefore, my beloved brethren, be ye steadfast, unmovable, always abounding in the work of the Lord, forasmuch as ye know that your labor is not in vain in the Lord."*

Romans 5:3-5: *"And not only so, but we glory in tribulations also: knowing that tribulation worketh patience; and patience, experience; and experience, hope: And hope maketh not ashamed; because the love of God is shed abroad in our hearts by the Holy Ghost which is given unto us."*

God has graciously given His people promises written in the Bible that we can remember when things are difficult. He is constantly encouraging us in the Psalms to think of Him in extra special ways. One special way God tells us to think of Him is as our Rock. Another special way we can think about God is as our Stronghold. These special names about God teach us to think about Him in times of hardship and difficulty. We learn to think about God in the pleasant times of life and in the not so pleasant times, too.

Do you have times that you think are difficult? Do you ever wonder why God has allowed hardship? Have you ever wondered about why God lets there be difficult and evil things happening around us?

God has allowed hard things and evil in this world for many reasons. One reason is that He wanted people to understand what they are really like on the inside. He also wanted people to see how desperately they need to be free from the power of sin working within them. He wants people to learn how much their sin offends Him. In the time of the Great Flood of Noah, God tells us in the Bible "evil abounded", and it was an offense to Him. However, God tells us that He had mercy on Noah and his family by giving them the plan for an ark that He would use to save them from the judgment on evil and sin that the Flood was going to be. In Genesis we learn that He did exactly what He planned.

Even after the Great Flood, God continued to allow hard things and evil in the world. He still wanted people like us to see what we are really like in our hearts and to understand our need for a Savior to free us from the power of sin that works within us. Sin and evil still offend God today and this offense always has to be dealt with. In His great mercy, God has given us the understanding of His plan to deal with the offense that our sins of any size have been to Him. It is in the Bible that we also learn that although God must deal with our sinfulness and the offense it brings Him, He chose to have mercy on us and to save us from the judgment that our sins deserve. His kind intention towards His people also included freeing us from the power of sin that works within us.

We learn from the Bible that God's plan for accomplishing these goals all centered on the life and death of Jesus Christ. God has told us in the Gospel that Jesus did everything God wanted Him to do. This perfect obedience to God even included suffering a horrible death on a Roman cross as a substitute for each of us. This means that Jesus took our sins upon Himself and suffered the judgment for them that we ought to have experienced. We understand that the Heavenly Father forgave us for our sins when He looked at Jesus suffering the punishment for them that we should have suffered. We understand that God also told us that we are right with Him because of Christ's sufferings in our place. This is how God dealt with the offense of our sins. Yet, His plan included more than this. God even sent His Holy Spirit as a gift to live in us as our source of power over sin. Amazed, we learn in the Gospel that God did even more for us and changed our hearts by the power of the Holy Spirit working in us so that we can love Him and the people, ideas, and things He loves!

Since God has saved us from experiencing the destruction and judgment that our sins honestly deserved, we could say Jesus Christ is like our Ark of Salvation. Since God has rescued us from the power of sin and sent the Holy Spirit to be our new source of power over any sin, we could say that Christ is also like our Rock of strength or power. A stronghold in Bible days was a place where people went to be safe from their enemies. We who know the reality of Jesus Christ understand that we can always go to Him in our times of trouble or hardship and be safe and secure in His Presence and care for us. We can even be steady and unmovable in the work that Christ has called us to do and in the trails of life because we know Him, our Rock and our Stronghold, who is also our Savior.

Knowing Christ as our Ark of Salvation, our Rock of strength over any sin, and our Stronghold in times of temptation and trouble gives us thankful hearts to God who has been so kind and generous to us. It also gives us hearts full of joy and love to know that God has loved us so mightily and that He created us and the world we live in for His pleasure, honor, and glory!